S0-BAF-321

Favorite Filipino Recipes

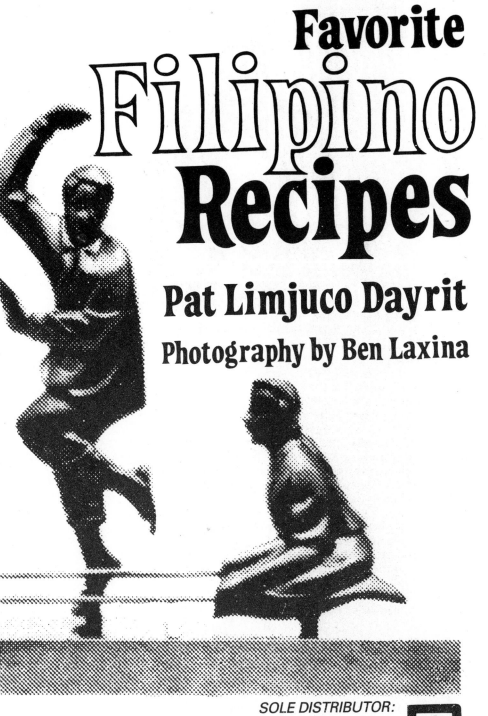

Favorite
Filipino
Recipes

Pat Limjuco Dayrit

Photography by Ben Laxina

SOLE DISTRIBUTOR:
Books for Pleasure Inc.
Rm. 302 First Optima Bldg.,
N. Domingo St. cor. F. Roman St.,
San Juan, Metro Manila

Books for Pleasure
Published by Paul Hamlyn Pty Limited
176 South Creek Road, Dee Why West, NSW, 2099
First published 1975
2nd impression 1977
3rd impression 1979
4th impression 1982
5th impression 1986
© Lansdowne Press 1975
Originated in the Philippines by the publisher
Line drawings by Christine Bruessow
Philippine artefacts used for chapter illustrations were
kindly loaned by Wengar & Co Pty Ltd,
Elizabeth Street, Sydney

Published & Distributed in the Philippines by:
Books for Pleasure, Inc.
Rm. 302 First Optima Bldg.,
N. Domingo St. cor. F. Roman St.,
San Juan, Metro Manila

Printed in the Philippines

All rights reserved. No part of this publication may be
reproduced, stored in a retrieval system, or transmitted
in any form or by any means, electronic, mechanical,
photocopying, recording, or otherwise, without the
prior permission of the publisher.

ISBN 971-502-009-7

Contents

Introduction

The recipes in this cookbook have been frequently tested in the 30 years that I have been cooking and teaching. They are the sum total of what the Filipinos eat — a potpourri of Spanish, American, Chinese, French, Japanese and Italian dishes — reflecting the varied cultural influences that have reached the country and its kitchens. Regional recipes have been included — the same recipe may be prepared differently in one home town from another.

The most important thing in cooking, I believe, is practice. The ingredients for preparing a good dish are ability, time and patience. The joy of cooking is there for those who enjoy it and the eating of the perfect roast, or stew, or cake, is its own ample reward.

Pat Limjuco Dayrit

Guide to Weights and Measures

For consistent results in cooking it is very important to weigh or measure carefully.

At the time of publication the quantities used throughout this book have been measured by volume in teaspoons, tablespoons or cups, according to the American standard as these are the available measures on the market. Where ingredients cannot be conveniently measured in cups or spoons, weight has been given. In many cases exact conversions cannot be given so approximations must be made, and after all many cooks, who rely on personal judgement for measuring, use their own taste skills to achieve certain flavorings or to present various food combinations. And so in the use of seasoning amounts in particular you should use your own judgement and vary the amount to suit your own, and/or your family's taste.

In general, references to measures follow that used in purchasing items on the market, which is a mixture of metric and imperial, e.g. kilos for meat, pounds for butter. With the gradual changeover to metric measures there are, and will be for some time, recipes which will include a mixture of both imperial and metric measurement with regard to amounts of ingredients to be used. Shops will continue to sell stock in its original size until stock is depleted. Where can sizes are given both imperial and metric sizes have been included because these weights will be marked on the cans and eventually with all new stock the size of the cans will change and the number of grams will be 'rounded off' according to an official metric standard.

An approximate guide to measures is given below.

1 teaspoon	— ⅓ tablespoon	— ⅙ fluid ounce	— 5 millilitres
3 teaspoons	— 1 tablespoon	— ½ fluid ounce	— 15 millilitres
2 tablespoons	— ⅛ cup		
4 tablespoons	— ¼ cup		
8 tablespoons	— ½ cup	— 4 fluid ounces	— 125 millilitres
16 tablespoons	— 1 cup	— 8 fluid ounces	— 250 millilitres
1 cup	— ½ pint		
2 cups	— 1 pint	— 16 fluid ounces	— 500 millilitres
4 cups	— 2 pints	— 1 litre	
2 pints	— 1 quart		
4 quarts	— 1 gallon		
½ pound	— 8 ounces	— 250 grams	
1 pound	— 16 ounces	— 500 grams	(0.5 kilogram)
1½ pounds	— 24 ounces	— 750 grams	
2 pounds	— 32 ounces	— 1000 grams	(1 kilogram)
3 pounds		— 1500 grams	(1.5 kilograms)
4 pounds		— 2000 grams	(2 kilograms)

Approximate can sizes and contents

6 oz can	— ¾ cup	— 185 grams
8 oz can	— 1 cup	— 250 grams
12 oz can	— 1½ cups	— 375 grams
16 oz can	— 2 cups	— 500 grams
20 oz can	— 2½ cups	— 625 grams
24 oz can	— 3 cups	— 750 grams

Abbreviations

oz	— ounce
lb	— pound
g	— gram
kg	— kilogram
kilos	— kilograms
ml	— millilitre
°F	— degrees Fahrenheit
°C	— degrees Centigrade

Oven Temperature Guide

This is an *approximate* guide only. Different makes of stoves vary and even the same make of stove can give slightly different individual results at the same temperature. If in doubt with your particular stove, do refer to your own manufacturer's temperature chart. It is impossible in a general book to be exact for every stove, but the following is a good average guide in every case. At present all ovens in the Philippines are in degrees Fahrenheit but as metric measures become more widely used it may be necessary to convert cooking temperatures to degrees Centigrade.

The following chart also gives approximate conversions from degrees Fahrenheit to degrees Centigrade. This chart can be used for conversion of recipes which give oven temperatures in metric measures.

Description of Oven	Thermostat Setting		
	°F		°C
	Automatic Electric	Gas	
Cool	200	200	90
Very slow	250	250	120
Slow	300-325	300	150-160
Moderately slow	325-350	325	160-170
Moderate	350-375	350	170-190
Moderately hot	375-400	375	190-200
Hot	400-450	400	200-230
Very hot	450-500	450	230-260

Soups

French onion soup

Serves: 6

4 tablespoons butter
2 tablespoons vegetable oil
2 cups chopped onion
salt and pepper to taste
1 teaspoon French mustard
2 tablespoons flour
4 cups beef stock and 1 can beef
consommé **or**
6 cups of beef stock and 2 beef
bouillon cubes
1 loaf French bread
grated parmesan cheese

Place butter and vegetable oil in a saucepan. Add onion, salt and pepper. Brown slowly over low heat for approximately 30 minutes. Add mustard and flour and stir until smooth. Continue stirring while adding stock until it is brought slowly to a boil. Simmer for 25 minutes. Pour into an earthenware casserole. Top with fine slices of French bread sprinkled with parmesan cheese and brown in the broiler. Serve at once.

Bam-i

Serves: 8

3 tablespoons cooking oil
6 cloves garlic, minced
1 small onion, chopped
3 tablespoons *patis*
8 cups chicken broth
½ cup *taingang daga*, soaked in water and cut into small pieces
¾ cup *singkamas*, cut in fine strips

1 kilo shredded boiled chicken, but use only the breast (native chicken preferred)
¼ kilo pork, cooked and cut into 2 x ¼" strips
300 grams *sotanghon*, soaked in water and cut
salt, pepper and vet-sin to taste

Sauté garlic and onion in hot cooking oil. Put in *patis* and bring to a boil. Add broth, *taingang daga, singkamas,* chicken, pork and *sotanghon.* Boil for 15 minutes until *sotanghon* is cooked. Season to taste with salt, pepper and vet-sin.

Sinampalocan manok

Serves: 8

1 chicken (1 to 1 ¼ kilos), cut into
serving pieces
salt
6 cloves garlic, crushed
1 tablespoon thinly sliced ginger
3 tablespoons lard
1 medium-sized onion, sliced
2 medium-sized ripe tomatoes,
chopped
2 cups tops of *sampaloc* leaves
2 tablespoons *patis*
8 cups water
1 teaspoon vet-sin (monosodium
glutamate)
salt and pepper for seasoning

Season the chicken pieces with salt. Set aside. Sauté garlic and ginger in lard. Add the onion and tomatoes, and cook until tomatoes are very soft. Add the chicken, turning it over until the liquid is almost dry.

Wrap *sampaloc* tops in a piece of cheesecloth and tie ends. Put *patis,* water and the wrapped *sampaloc* tops in with the chicken. Simmer 30 to 40 minutes or until the chicken is tender. Add vet-sin and correct seasoning. Remove wrapped *sampaloc* tops before serving.

Pancit molo

Serves: 12

Wrapper
1 cup flour
¼ teaspoon salt
2 egg yolks
enough water to make a paste

Place flour and salt on a slab or in a bowl. Make a well in the center and add eggs and water. Work it up to a paste and knead until smooth. Roll paper thin with cornstarch and cut into triangles 3 inches on two sides, shorter on one side.

HOW TO WRAP PANCIT MOLO:

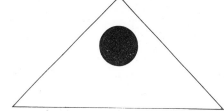

1. Place meat mixture on one corner of triangular molo wrapper.

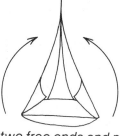

4. Take up two free ends and press them firmly together with a little water.

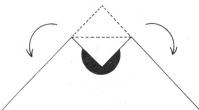

2. Fold one corner of wrapper.

3. Fold it another time, and a third time.

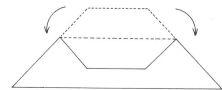

14

Filling

⅓ kilo ground pork
3 tablespoons shrimps, chopped
½ cup finely chopped *apulid*, or
singkamas
2 tablespoons chopped spring onions
3 dried Chinese mushrooms, soaked
in water and chopped
2 tablespoons soy sauce
1 teaspoon vet-sin (monosodium
glutamate)
1 egg
2 dashes of sesame oil
salt and pepper

Combine all ingredients of the filling and wrap into the *wanton* wrappers you have made. Place a teaspoon of the 'mixture' at one angle of the triangle-shaped wrapper and wrap, rolling and joining the tips, as illustrated.

Broth

3 cloves garlic, crushed
1 medium-sized onion, chopped
3 tablespoons cooking oil
½ kilo shrimps, shelled and de-veined
4 tablespoons *patis*
salt and pepper to taste
1 teaspoon vet-sin (monosodium
glutamate)
12 cups chicken broth
1 breast of boiled chicken, flaked
3 tablespoons chopped spring onions

Sauté the garlic and onion in cooking oil. Add shrimps and season with *patis*, salt, pepper and vet-sin. Cook until fishy taste is removed. Pour in broth and flaked chicken and bring to a boil. Drop in the stuffed wrappers and boil for 15 minutes. Pour in a soup bowl and sprinkle with freshly chopped spring onions.

Chicken binakol
(See photograph on page 17)

Serves: 8

3 tablespoons lard
6 cloves garlic, crushed
1 medium-sized onion, chopped
1 tablespoon thinly sliced ginger
3 tablespoons *patis*
1 chicken (about 1 kilo), deboned
and sliced thinly, 1 inch square
6 cups chicken stock (made from
chicken bones)
1 *buko*, cut into bite-size pieces
(save water)
salt and pepper to taste
1 teaspoon vet-sin (monosodium
glutamate)

Sauté garlic, onion, and ginger in lard. Add *patis* and let boil. Add chicken and stir, then pour in the chicken stock. Simmer 30 minutes or until the chicken is tender. Add the *buko* water and meat. Season with salt, pepper and vet-sin.

Chicken Binakol (see recipe opposite)

Lobster Thermidor (see recipe on page 23)

Bachoy

Serves: 6

300 grams pork kidney
¼ kilo pork *lapáy*
¼ kilo pork tenderloin
4 cloves garlic, crushed
1 medium-sized onion, chopped
1 tablespoon ginger, cut into fine
·strips
3 tablespoons *patis*
5 cups water
salt and pepper to taste
1 teaspoon vet-sin (monosodium
glutamate)
200 grams pork brains (about 2)
(optional)

Cut open kidney and remove the white parts from inside which if left in will give it a slight odor. Rub kidney with salt and wash thoroughly. Slice kidney, *lapáy*, and pork tenderloin into ¾ inch squares as thinly as possible. Set aside.

In cooking oil sauté garlic, onion, ginger and *patis*. When onion is transparent, put in the *lapáy* and kidneys. Stir about 10 minutes. Add pork tenderloin and stir about 2 minutes more. Add water and bring to a boil. Season with salt, pepper and vet-sin. Simmer 5 minutes.

Remove membrane from the brain and cut into 1 inch pieces. Add to the soup. Boil 2 minutes and serve hot.

Sopa de ajo

(Garlic Soup)

Serves: 4

3 pieces *pan de sal* or an 8 inch
French bread stick
6 tablespoons olive oil
1 tablespoon chopped garlic
2 tablespoons chopped onion
4 cups chicken broth
salt and pepper to taste
1 teaspoon, vet-sin (monosodium
glutamate)
bread slices
4 eggs

Slice the *pan de sal* ¼ inch thick crosswise, and toast. Set aside. Heat olive oil in a saucepan and add the garlic and onion. Stir for a few minutes without browning. Add broth, salt, pepper and vet-sin and let boil. Ladle into soup plates, putting a few slices of bread and one egg in each. Serve at once.

Fish and Seafood

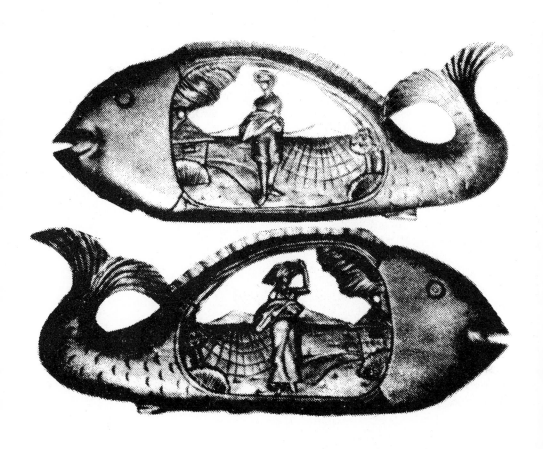

Tortilla de cangrejo

Serves: 8

3 large crabs
2 cups chopped cabbage (cut into 1 inch pieces)
2 tablespoons lard for sautéeing
1 large onion, sliced
2 pieces dried Chinese mushrooms, cut into thin strips
10 apulid or singkamas, cut into 1/8 inch thick slices
1/4 kilo shrimps
1 teaspoon oyster sauce
1 tablespoon soy sauce
1 teaspoon vet-sin (monosodium glutamate)
salt and pepper to taste
1 medium-sized patola (cut into 1 1/2 inch wedges)
3 dashes sesame oil
3 eggs for every omelet (recipe makes 3-4 omelets)
salt and pepper to taste
lard for frying

Boil and peel crabs and flake the meat. Set aside. Place the cabbage in a little hot lard for about two minutes. Remove and set aside. In the same hot lard, put in onion and stir for two minutes. Add the mushrooms, the apulid (or singkamas), then the crabs and shrimps. Flavor with oyster sauce, soy sauce, vet-sin, salt and pepper. Add the patola and the cabbage and boil once. Sprinkle with three dashes sesame oil.

Remove from heat. Strain and set liquid aside. Divide mixture into 3 or 4 parts to make 3 or 4 omelets (tortillas). For each omelet beat 3 eggs slightly. Put in salt and pepper.

Heat 2 teaspoons oil for each omelet. When hot, pour slightly beaten eggs to spread out over pan. When set, put filling on one side so you can fold over the other side. Remove from heat.

Serve with sweet and sour sauce (see below).

Sweet and sour sauce
1 tablespoon cider vinegar
3 tablespoons sugar
1/2 cup water
1/2 teaspoon salt
1 teaspoon oyster sauce
1 tablespoon catsup
1 tablespoon cornstarch
2 tablespoons water

Combine vinegar, sugar, water, salt, oyster sauce and catsup. Add the strained sauce of the filling. Boil and thicken with cornstarch dissolved in water.

Lobster thermidor

(See photograph on page 18)

Serves: 8

2 fresh lobsters (½ kilo each), or
about ¾ kilo prawns (10-12 pieces)
4 tablespoons cooking oil
2 medium-sized onions, chopped
4 tablespoons butter
¼ cup dry white wine
2 tablespoons flour
¾ cup milk
½ cup cream
1 teaspoon French mustard
⅓ cup of grated cheese
dash or two of cayenne pepper
salt and vet-sin (monosodium glutamate) to taste

Wash the lobsters in cold water, split in half and put in the pan, shell side down. Fry in oil for 15 minutes. Remove lobster meat from the shell and cut up roughly. If prawns are used, fry them whole — slit open the shell at the back. Remove meat and cut roughly.

Cook onions in 2 tablespoons butter without browning, then pour in white wine. Cook until wine has evaporated.

In another pan melt 2 tablespoons butter. Remove from heat. Add flour and mix thoroughly. Pour in the milk gradually. Return to heat. Stir over the fire until it thickens then add cream, French mustard, and grated cheese. Mix in the lobster or prawn meat and onion. Season with cayenne pepper, salt and vet-sin. Fill the shells with this mixture. Sprinkle with grated cheese, dot with butter and brown in the broiler.

Crab sautéed with tausi sauce

Serves: 4

2 big fresh crabs
pepper and salt
1 teaspoon minced ginger
2 tablespoons cornstarch
cooking oil for deep frying
2 cloves garlic, chopped
2 tablespoons *tausi*

1 large hot pepper, sliced (not *labuyo*)
½ tablespoon sugar
1 tablespoon Chinese wine (*sioktong*)
1 cup water
½ teaspoon sesame oil

Cut the crab into 4 pieces and clean thoroughly. Include the claws, cracking them first. Drain crab meat and mix with pepper, salt, ginger and cornstarch. Heat cooking oil and fry crab about 5 minutes or until half cooked. Remove and drain.

Use about 2 tablespoons of the remaining cooking oil to fry the garlic, *tausi*, hot pepper and sugar. Add the crab, Chinese wine and water, then cover and simmer for 20 minutes or until the liquid has evaporated. Add sesame oil and serve.

Tortilla de camarron

Serves: 4

½ kilo shrimps, chopped
1 medium-sized onion, chopped
3 tablespoons chopped *kinchay* stems
2 tablespoons chopped spring onions
2 eggs
crushed peppercorns and salt to taste
lard for frying

Combine all ingredients except the eggs. Season with salt and peppercorns. Beat eggs until thick. Fold into mixture. Heat 1 tablespoon lard in a frying pan. Drop the mixture by the tablespoon and fry until the *tortillas* are golden brown.

Drain *tortillas* and serve with catsup, or salad made of thinly sliced radishes with dressing of vinegar, salt and sugar.

Camarron rellenado

Serves: 8

1 kilo large shrimps (about 35 pieces)
¼ kilo *apulid*, or 1 small *singkamas*, cut into match-like strips
6 Chinese mushrooms, cut into fine strips
¼ kilo pork fat, cut into fine strips
1 small carrot, cut into fine strips
¾ cup chopped spring onions, chopped into 1 inch lengths
½ cup ham, cut into fine strips

salt and pepper to taste
1 teaspoon vet-sin (monosodium glutamate)
3 tablespoons soy sauce
2 tablespoons sugar
2 egg yolks
2 tablespoons cornstarch
2 dashes sesame oil
batter (see below)
½ kilo *untosinsal*, or leaf lard

Peel the shrimps keeping the tail intact. Slit the backs of the shrimps so they will open up. Remove black veins. Wash and season with salt. Combine the *apulid*, mushrooms, pork fat, carrot, spring onions and ham. Season with salt, pepper, vet-sin, soy sauce and sugar. Add the egg yolks, cornstarch and sesame oil.

Make a batter of ¼ cup water, ¼ cup eggwhite, ¾ cup cornstarch and ½ teaspoon salt.

Enclose each shrimp in a tablespoon of the filling and wrap with a piece of *untosinsal*, or leaf lard. Dip each wrapped shrimp into the batter and fry in deep fat until golden brown.

Serve with sweet and sour radish, described in recipe for *Kue Kiam* (see page 57).

Stuffed fish fillets

(See photograph on page 53)

Serves: 8

1½ kilo red *lapulapu* (about 14 fillets 2 x 4 inches)
2 *calamansi*, or 1 slice of lemon
½ kilo cooked shrimps
2 egg yolks
salt and pepper
14 strips of ham
(about 2 x ¼ inches)
14 strips of pickles
(about 2 x ¼ inches)
14 strips of carrots
(about 2 x ½ inches)
3 hard boiled eggs, sliced lengthwise into 8 wedges

3 tablespoons port wine, or sherry
1 stalk celery, cut into 2 inch pieces
2 sprigs parsley
1 medium-sized onion, sliced
3 tablespoons butter
salt to taste
1 tablespoon peppercorns
1½ cups cooked and diced stringbeans
1½ cups diced cooked carrots
extra salt and pepper for seasoning sauce (see below)

Wash fillets well and squeeze *calamansi* or lemon juice over the fish. Season with salt and pepper. Set aside. Chop shrimps, add egg yolks, salt and pepper. Spread a layer of this on each fillet. In the center of the fillet put strips of ham, pickles, carrots and hard boiled eggs. Roll up each fillet with its filling. Wrap in aluminium foil.

In a saucepan, place the head and tail of the fish. Add wine or sherry, celery, parsley, onion, butter, salt and peppercorns. Bring to a boil. Add the wrapped fish fillets and allow to boil for 20 minutes. Remove the wrappers and cut each stuffed fillet into two crosswise to exhibit the colorful filling.

Arrange on the serving dish cut side up. For decoration, sauté diced green beans and carrots separately in butter. Season with salt and pepper. Arrange alternately by the tablespoon around the fillets. Serve with the following sauce.

Sauce
2 tablespoons butter
2 tablespoons toasted flour
1½ cups fish stock
2 tablespoons grated cheese
salt
1 teaspoon vet-sin (monosodium glutamate)

26

Melt the butter in a saucepan. Remove from heat and add toasted flour and strained fish stock. Stir over the heat until mixture thickens, then add grated cheese. Season with salt and vet-sin to taste.

Vinegrettes soufflé

Serves: 8

2 tablespoons butter
½ cup water
½ cup all-purpose flour
½ teaspoon salt
2 eggs
½ teaspoon baking powder
¼ cup egg whites
3 slices bacon, fried and chopped
½ cup grated Edam cheese (*queso de bola*)
⅓ kilo fresh shrimps, peeled and chopped

1 medium-sized onion, chopped
3 tablespoons chopped spring onions
3 tablespoons chopped Chinese celery
salt and pepper to taste
½ teaspoon vet-sin (monosodium glutamate)
lard for deep frying

Place butter and water in a pan. When bubbling add the flour and salt beating until it forms a ball in the pan. Beat the eggs off the fire, then add to the mixture in the pan, one at a time, beating well after each addition.

Add baking powder and fold in stiffly beaten egg whites. Divide into 4 parts. To one part add the bacon. To other part add cheese. To the two remaining parts add the shrimps, bulb onion and spring onions, Chinese celery, salt, pepper and vet-sin.

Heat lard. Drop in ¼ teaspoon balls of bacon and cheese mixture, and ½ teaspoon balls of shrimp mixture. Deep fry.

Rellenong bangus

Serves: 5

½ kilo *bangus*
2 tablespoons soy sauce
juice of 2 *calamansi*, or 1 lemon
pinch of salt
3 tablespoons lard
4 cloves garlic, chopped
1 medium-sized onion, chopped
½ kilo ground pork

1 potato, peeled, diced and fried
¼ cup raisins
¼ cup frozen peas
salt and pepper for seasoning
2 eggs
enough flour to cover fish
extra lard for frying
parsley and tomatoes for garnish

Remove the scales and wash fish thoroughly. Slit the back and scrape out all the flesh. Soak the skin in soy sauce and *calamansi* or lemon juice for about 10 minutes.

Boil the fish flesh with a little water and a pinch of salt. Drain and pick out the spines. Heat the lard and sauté the garlic and onions. Add the pork and cook for five minutes. Add the flaked fish and cook for another five minutes. Removed from heat and add fried potatoes, raisins and peas. Season with salt, pepper and extra *calamansi* or lemon juice. Add the eggs and mix.

Fill the whole skin of the fish with this stuffing and sew the slit with needle and thread. Dredge in flour. Fry in hot lard until golden brown. Place on a platter and decorate with parsley and tomato slices.

Lapulapu with tausi

Serves: 6

2 slices ginger
2 tablespoons water
½ kilo *lapulapu* fillets
salt and pepper to taste
lard for frying
1 x 4 inch square *tauhu*, cut into
1 x 1½ inch slices
1 tablespoon chopped spring onions,
cut in 1 inch lengths
1 tablespoon ginger, cut into fine
strips

4 tablespoons *tausi*, or black beans
(canned, or by the kilo from Chinese
groceries)
1½ cups water
2 tablespoons cornstarch dissolved
in water
3 medium-sized onions, cut in
wedges
3 medium-sized tomatoes, cut in
wedges
dash of sesame oil

Crush the ginger and add water. Soak fillets in ginger juice for a few minutes. Wash, and season with salt and pepper. Roll in cornstarch and fry in lard until light brown. Fry *tauhu*. Set aside.

Remove some of the left-over lard, then sauté spring onions and ginger in the same pan. Add the *tausi* and water. Thicken with the cornstarch, stirring vigorously. Place the *lapulapu* fillets, *tauhu*, onions and tomatoes into the pan. Boil once. Sprinkle with sesame oil and serve.

Adobong pusit

Serves: 4

½ kilo small fresh squids
½ cup native vinegar
10 cloves garlic
salt and pepper to taste
1 medium-sized onion, sliced
2 medium-sized tomatoes, chopped
extra salt and pepper for seasoning
1 teaspoon vet-sin (monosodium glutamate)

Wash the squids very well. Remove the long thin membrane in the head and slit the eyes to bring out the ink. Place squids in a saucepan with vinegar, 6 cloves garlic crushed, salt and pepper. Cover and cook slowly until squids are tender. Cut cooked squids into ½ inch slices crosswise.

Crush remaining garlic and sauté in a little lard in another pan. Add the onion and tomatoes and cook until tomatoes are very soft. Add the squids and the liquid in which they were boiled. Simmer for 7 minutes. Season with salt, pepper and vet-sin.

Rellenong alimasag

Serves: 8

1 kilo *alimasag* (crabs)
lard for frying
2 peeled potatoes, finely diced
6 cloves garlic, crushed
1 onion, chopped
2 peeled tomatoes, chopped
salt and pepper
2 eggs
3 tablespoons (approx.) lard

Boil and flake crabs (save top shells). Fry diced potatoes and set aside. Heat lard and sauté garlic until brown. Add onion and tomatoes, crushing them well. Then add crabmeat and potatoes, season with salt and pepper and cook for a few minutes. Fill crab shells with this mixture.

Beat eggs until thick. Heat 1 tablespoon lard in a frying pan and put in 2 tablespoons of the beaten egg. When set, place the filled crab shell carefully upside down on the egg and fry quickly. Repeat with every crab shell.

Note: approximately 1 tablespoon lard for each filled crab shell.

Prawn ravigote

(See photograph on page 35)

Serves: 8-10

12-14 prawns (1 kilo)
5 medium-sized tomatoes (seeds removed), diced ½ inch
2 tablespoons chopped spring onions
½ cup finely diced celery
⅓ cup finely diced sweet pickles
1 cup mayonnaise
salt and pepper
a little lemon juice
2 hard boiled eggs
parsley and lemon slices for garnish

Boil prawns and slit the shell at the back. Remove the meat carefully and cut roughly into ½ inch cubes. Save shells. Mix prawn meat with tomatoes, spring onions, celery and sweet pickles. Add mayonnaise and season with salt, pepper and lemon juice.

Fill shells with this mixture and lightly cover with mayonnaise. Sprinkle with chopped hard boiled eggs, arrange on a platter and decorate with parsley and slices of lemon.

Lagat na hipon

Serves: 4

½ kilo shrimps
¼ cup native vinegar
2 medium-sized onions, sliced
salt to taste
½ teaspoon crushed peppercorns
4 cloves garlic, crushed
3 tablespoons lard
8 kamias, sliced crosswise
(approximately ¼ inch thick)

Peel the shrimps and wash them. Place shrimps in mixture of vinegar, onions, salt and peppercorns. Set aside.

Sauté the crushed garlic in the lard and add the shrimp mixture. Stir well when it starts boiling (not before as it will taste vinegary). Cook until shrimps turn red. Add the kamias and bring to the boil.

Pescado al horno

(Baked lapulapu)

Serves: 6

½ kilo lapulapu (6 to 8 fillets)
2 calamansi, or 1 slice of lemon
salt and pepper for seasoning
⅓ cup of olive oil
1 medium-sized onion, sliced
1 x 245 grams can whole tomatoes
½ cup pimento, cut into ¼ x 3 inch strips
1 tablespoon chopped parsley
1 tablespoon breadcrumbs

Wash fillets with *calamansi* or lemon juice and water. Arrange in a Pyrex dish. Season with salt and pepper.

Heat olive oil in a pan for the sauce. Add the onion and the tomatoes. Season with salt and pepper and add the *pimento*.

Pour sauce over the fish, sprinkle with chopped parsley and breadcrumbs. Bake at 350°F for 25 minutes.

Shrimp croquettes

Serves: 6

3 tablespoons lard
3 cloves garlic
1 small onion, chopped
¼ cup tomato sauce
½ cup shrimps, chopped
salt and pepper to taste
mashed potatoes (see below)
¾ cup flour
2 beaten eggs
1 cup breadcrumbs

Sauté garlic and onion in lard. Pour in the tomato sauce. After a while, add the shrimps. Cook well to remove fishy taste. Season with salt and pepper.

Put a tablespoon of the mixture in the center of sufficient mashed potatoes to form into small egg-like balls. Roll balls in flour and dip in beaten eggs. Coat with breadcrumbs. Fry in deep fat until golden-brown.

Mashed potatoes
1 kilo potatoes
2 egg yolks
4 tablespoons butter
salt and pepper to taste

Boil the potatoes until soft. Peel and pass thru a sieve. Add egg yolks and butter. Season with salt and pepper.

Camarron dorado con jamon

Serves: 8

1 kilo large shrimps (not less than 3 inches long)
3 slices ginger
3 tablespoons water
1 teaspoon salt
¼ cup egg white
¼ cup water
1 teaspoon vet-sin (monosodium glutamate)

25-30 pieces pork fat, sliced (about 1 x 1½ inches)
25-30 pieces ham, sliced (about 1 x 1½ inches)
¼ cup flour
¾ cup cornstarch
lard for deep frying
sweet and sour sauce (see below)

Peel the shrimps and slit them deeply at the back so that they open wide. Remove veins and wash.

Crush the ginger and add water. Place the shrimps in this juice and set aside for 3 minutes. Remove ginger juice and wash shrimps again. Beat egg white slightly and add water, vet-sin, salt, flour and cornstarch. Note: This batter should be thick and lumpy. Do not over beat.

Dip shrimps in this batter mixture, one by one. In a spoon, place a slice of pork fat, and a shrimp which has been dipped in the batter. If shrimp is big it can be folded so that it forms a rectangle. Top shrimp with slice of ham and a little of the batter. Push it carefully with a fork into the hot lard so that it does not get disarranged. Fry until golden brown. Serve with sweet and sour sauce.

Sweet and sour sauce
2 tablespoons cider vinegar
6 tablespoons sugar
1 cup water
½ teaspoon salt
1 teaspoon oyster sauce
1 tablespoon catsup
1 rounded tablespoon cornstarch dissolved in a little water

Combine all the sauce ingredients except cornstarch. Bring to the boil, pour in cornstarch and stir vigorously. Serve hot.

Prawn Ravigote (see recipe on page 31)

Fisherman's Dream (see recipe opposite)

Fisherman's dream

(See photograph opposite)

Serves: 10

1½ kilos *apahap*, or *lapulapu*
2 *calamansi*, or 1 slice of lemon
salt and pepper to taste
2 medium-sized onions, chopped
2 medium-sized tomatoes, chopped
4 tablespoons white wine
½ cup olive oil
1½ cups water
⅓ cup grated cheese

2 tablespoons butter
extra salt and pepper for seasoning
sauce (see below)
1 medium-sized boiled beet,
chopped
1 medium-sized boiled carrot,
chopped
4 tablespoons chopped sweet pickle
relish, or sweet pickles

Scale and clean fish thoroughly. Cut diagonal slashes on sides of fish. Dredge with *calamansi* or lemon juice, salt and pepper. In a baking dish arrange onions and tomatoes, and lay the fish on them. Put in the wine, olive oil, and water. Sprinkle grated cheese on top of the fish and dot with butter. Season with a little salt and pepper.

Bake at 350°F for 45 minutes to one hour. When done, place fish on a serving dish and pour the sauce over it. Decorate with chopped beets in a 1 inch band across the fish. Alternate with band of chopped carrots and band of chopped pickles.

Sauce
2 tablespoons butter
2 tablespoons toasted flour
1½ cups fish stock
salt, pepper and ½ teaspoon vet-sin
(monosodium glutamate)
2 tablespoons grated cheese

Melt butter in pan. Remove from heat. Add toasted flour and strained fish stock. Season with salt, pepper and vet-sin. Stir over low heat until slightly thick. Add grated cheese and pour sauce over fish just before serving.

Pescado con salsa blanca

Serves: 8-10

1 *apahap*, or *lapulapu* (1-1½ kilos)
2 *calamansi*, or 1 slice lemon
salt and pepper to taste
1 medium-sized onion, sliced
crosswise
1 medium-sized tomato, sliced
3 tablespoons white wine
4 pieces celery, or *kinchay*, cut into
1 inch pieces
1½ cups water
2 tablespoons butter
2 tablespoons flour
⅓ cup evaporated milk
salt and pepper to taste

Clean fish thoroughly, squeezing *calamansi* or lemon inside and outside the fish. Place in baking dish and season with salt and pepper. Add onion, tomato, white wine, celery or *kinchay* and water. Bake in a 350°F oven for about 40 or 50 minutes (or until cooked). Remove from heat and strain sauce.

In another pan, melt butter. Remove from fire and add flour and the sauce of the fish. Cook over a low fire until thick and add milk. Season with salt and pepper. Continue cooking until sauce is thick (sauce should be thinner, however, than white sauce). Pour over the fish just before serving.

Meats and Poultry

Beef Stroganoff

Serves: 4

500 grams beef tenderloin
butter for browning
3 tablespoons sherry
2 tablespoons butter
1 teaspoon chopped garlic
1 medium-sized onion, chopped
1 teaspoon tomato paste
4 tablespoons flour
1¼ cups broth
⅓ cup sour cream
salt, pepper, vet-sin (monosodium glutamate)
4 oz (125 g) egg noodles

Cut beef tenderloin into 3 x ½ inch slices. Brown very quickly in hot butter. Remove beef.

Put into the pan hot sherry, butter, garlic and onion. Cook for 1 minute. Add tomato paste, flour and broth. Stir over the heat until boiling. Add sour cream, salt, pepper and vet-sin. Put back beef and cook 3 minutes. Serve with noodles.

Pato tim

Serves: 4

1 duck (about 1¼ kilos)
2 tablespoons Chinese wine (sioktong)
3 tablespoons soy sauce
1 small piece of ginger, crushed
lard for frying
6 pieces Chinese mushrooms, soaked in water
spring onions, cut in half, ends split into 4 and opened up

2 slices ginger
¼ teaspoon Ngo Yong powder
asparagus stock, from 8 oz (250 grams) can
3 tablespoons AA-gaugau
3 tablespoons water
1 x 8 oz (250 grams) can asparagus tips

Clean duck thoroughly. Make a marinade of Chinese wine, soy sauce and ginger. Soak the duck in this the day before.

Just before cooking, drain and brush the duck with more soy sauce. Brown in a little lard. Place in a pan with the Chinese mushrooms, the 2 ginger slices and *Ngo-Yong* powder. Steam 3 hours or until duck is tender. Take duck's drippings from the pan. Add asparagus stock drained from asparagus tips. Thicken with AA-*gaugau* dissolved in a little water.

Put duck on a serving dish. Remove the bones by slitting the back of the duck. (The duck is very tender and the bones are easily removed). Turn the duck over and pour on sauce. Decorate with asparagus tips and spring onions before serving.

Mechado

Serves: 6

1½ kilos *kabilugan*, larded
juice of 2-3 *calamansi*
4 to 5 tablespoons soy sauce
1 large onion, sliced
3 cloves of garlic, crushed
3 tablespoons sherry
1½ cups water
salt and peppercorns
1 small bay leaf
2-3 tablespoons all-purpose flour
2 tablespoons butter
3 potatoes, peeled and quartered

The day before, soak the beef in a little *calamansi* juice and soy sauce. Reserve the marinade.

The next day brown the meat in a little lard then add the onion, garlic, sherry, water, salt, peppercorns, bay leaf, and simmer until tender.

Remove meat from pan, slice and strain sauce. Thicken with a little toasted flour and butter. Return meat and add the potatoes. Simmer until tender.

Callos

Serves: 12

1 medium-sized ox *pata* (about
1½ kilos)
1 kilo tripe (packaged: cleaned and
precooked)
½ cup ham
2 *chorizo de Bilbao*
½ cup olive oil
1 medium-sized onion, chopped
½ cup tomato sauce
1 cup *garbanzos*
2 cups broth

3 tablespoons sherry
½ bay leaf
salt
1 teaspoon crushed peppercorns
1 teaspoon vet-sin (monosodium
glutamate)
1 cup *pimento*
1 cup green olives
2 tablespoons flour
¼ cup water

Boil the ox *pata* and discard water. Boil again together with tripe until tender.
Save broth. Cut *pata*, tripe, ham and *chorizo* into 1 inch pieces. Set aside.

Heat olive oil in a pan. Add onion and cook until soft, then add tomato sauce
and bring to a boil. Add the ham, tripe, ox *pata*, *chorizo* and *garbanzos*. When
boiling add the broth, sherry, and bay leaf. Season with salt, peppercorns and
vet-sin. Add the *pimento* and the olives. Thicken sauce with a little flour
dissolved in small amount of water.

Chicken à la Kiev

Serves: 4

2 chickens (1 kilo each)
1 lump firm fresh butter (about
3 x ⅔ x ¾ inches)
1 teaspoon chopped garlic
1 teaspoon finely chopped parsley
salt and pepper
½ cup all-purpose flour

1 egg
1 cup breadcrumbs
2 cups cooking oil
½ kilo potatoes, French-fried for
decoration
some parsley, *pimento* for decoration

Separate the breast of the chickens from the bones and carefully take off the skin. Cut breasts in half and place each piece between 2 pieces of wax paper. Beat with a mallet until thin. In the center of each chicken piece, place a lump of firm butter, ¼ teaspoon garlic and ¼ teaspoon chopped parsley. Season with salt and pepper to taste.

Roll up chicken breasts, tucking in each end. Dust with flour and brush with beaten egg. Dust with flour and brush with beaten egg again. Roll breasts in breadcrumbs. Fry in hot oil for approx. 3 minutes until golden brown.

Insert a cocktail stick covered with colored cellophane frills at end of each breast roll and arrange rolls on a serving dish. Decorate with French-fried potatoes, parsley and *pimento*. (The bone of the drumstick may be stuck into one end to simulate a leg.)

Pochero

Serves: 8

1 chicken (1 kilo)
½ kilo pork, cut into serving pieces
½ kilo cooked beef (*kenchie*)
4 tablespoons olive oil or lard
6 cloves garlic
1 medium-sized onion, sliced
⅔ can tomato sauce
2 cups broth
3 potatoes, peeled and quartered
6 pieces *saba* bananas

1 piece *chorizo de Bilbao* (if imported); 3 pieces (if Purefoods)
1 cup *garbanzos*, boiled
1 small cabbage, quartered
$^1/_8$ kilo string beans
2 heads *pechay*
salt and pepper to taste
1 teaspoon vet-sin (monosodium glutamate)
2 tablespoons flour (approx.)

Boil chicken, pork and beef until tender. Sauté garlic in hot oil, add onion and tomato sauce. Bring to a boil. Pour in broth and simmer for 15 minutes.

Put in the potatoes, bananas, *chorizo de Bilbao* and *garbanzos*. Simmer until potatoes and bananas are tender. Add cabbage, string beans and *pechay*. Put in meat and chicken. Continue simmering until string beans are cooked. Season with salt, pepper and vet-sin. If necessary thicken sauce with flour dissolved in water.

Paksiw na lechon

Serves: 6

1 kilo *lechon*
1½ cups *lechon* sauce
½ laurel leaf
1 head garlic
4 tablespoons brown sugar
2 stems of oregano
peppercorns
salt

Combine all ingredients in a saucepan and simmer for about half an hour over low heat. Cook until tender.

Chicken galantina

Serves: 12

1 chicken (about 1½ kilos)
salt and pepper
⅓ kilo ground pork
1 Oxford sausage, or 2 x 145 grams cans Vienna sausage
1 small can pâté de foie-gras
5 eggs
½ cup chopped sweet pickles
⅔ cup grated Edam cheese (*queso de bola*)
salt and pepper
1 teaspoon vet-sin (monosodium glutamate)
2 tablespoons butter
2 hard boiled eggs
1 carrot, cut into 3 x ½ inch strips
2 cups chicken broth
1 piece sweet pickle, quartered lengthwise

Cut the neck, the big joints of the wings and the top of the leg joints of the chicken. Turn over and slit the back. Remove the leg bones and the wing bones. Remove all dark meat from the bones, but not the white meat. Avoid splitting the skin. Spread chicken on a board. Season with salt and pepper.

Chop the dark meat and add pork, Oxford or Vienna sausage (if latter, reserve 3), pâté, raw eggs, pickles, cheese, salt, pepper, vet-sin, and butter. Fill the chicken with this mixture. Place in the center of it hard boiled eggs quartered lengthwise, also carrot, the rest of the sweet pickles and the 3 pieces Vienna sausage, halved lengthwise.

Roll the chicken carefully and sew the opening at the back. Wrap in aluminum foil. Cook in good chicken broth for about 1 hour. When cooked, cool in the refrigerator. Cut into halves and then into thin slices. Serve cold with salad.

Fritada

Serves: 6

1 chicken (about 1 kilo)
½ kilo pork
salt and pepper to taste
flour
lard
4 cloves garlic, crushed
1 medium-sized onion, chopped
1 medium-sized tomato, chopped
½ x 8 oz (250 grams) can tomato sauce
2 cups water

1 small bay leaf
1 sprig oregano
1 green or red bell pepper, cut into 1 inch squares
4 medium-sized potatoes, cut into 2 inch pieces
flour for thickening
½ cup frozen peas
½ x 200 grams can *pimento*, cut into 1 inch squares

Cut the chicken into serving pieces. Cut the pork into 1½ inch squares. Dredge with salt, pepper, and flour, and brown quickly in hot lard.

Sauté garlic and add onion, tomato and tomato sauce. Pour in the water and let boil. Add the chicken, pork, bay leaf, oregano, and green or red pepper. Simmer for 30 minutes, or until tender. Add potatoes and cook until tender. Correct the seasoning.

Thicken the sauce with flour dissolved in a little water. Add peas and *pimento*. Cook 3 more minutes.

Poulet au riz

Serves: 4

Chicken
1 chicken (1-1¼ kilo)
4 tablespoons butter
2 tablespoons all-purpose flour
¼ cup chicken stock, or water
sprig of parsley
1 medium-sized onion, sliced
1 stem celery, cut into 2 inch pieces
salt and pepper to taste

Sauce
2 egg yolks
½ teaspoon lemon juice
4 tablespoons evaporated milk
salt and cayenne pepper to taste
4 tablespoons butter
1 tablespoon grated Edam cheese
(*queso de bola*)

Rice
3 tablespoons butter
1 small onion, chopped
½ teaspoon *pimenton* (red pepper),
or paprika
3 cups water, or chicken stock
1¼ cups uncooked packaged
American rice
1 red *pimento*, diced
salt and pepper to taste

Brown the chicken in two tablespoons butter. Set aside. In another pan, melt two tablespoons butter. Remove from heat and add flour and the chicken stock or water. Return to heat and stir until boiling, than add the chicken, parsley, onion, celery, salt and pepper. Simmer until chicken is tender, or for about 45 minutes to one hour. Strain liquid and save for sauce.

To make sauce
Put the egg yolks, lemon juice, milk, salt and cayenne pepper in a Pyrex bowl. Beat over another pan of hot water set over the fire. When thick, add the butter gradually. Add the strained liquid (from the cooking of the chicken) and grated cheese.

To cook rice
Heat butter in a saucepan, add the onion and the *pimenton* or paprika. Stir until onion is soft then add the rice and blend well. Add water or chicken stock. Boil for three minutes, then simmer until rice is cooked, or for about 15 minutes. Add *pimento* and season with salt and pepper.

To serve
Mould rice in a greased ring mould and turn over on a round platter. Cut chicken into serving pieces and arrange in the middle and sides of moulded rice. Pour sauce over chicken and serve.

Sinigang na carne

Serves: 6-8

½ kilo cheaper cuts of beef with bones (*panigang*)
½ kilo pork spareribs
6 cups water in which rice has been washed the second time
3 tomatoes, sliced
1 medium-sized onion, sliced
8 fresh *kamias*

patis to taste
vet-sin (monosodium glutamate)
3 *gabi*, cut into 1½ inch cubes
3 radishes, cut at an angle into ⅓ inch slices
2 cups *kangkong*, or mustard leaves, cut into 2 inch pieces
2 *sili, panigang* variety

Simmer beef and pork in rice washing water. Add sliced tomatoes, onion and *kamias*. Crush *kamias* when soft and put back into the broth. Add *patis* and vet-sin to broth. When meat gets tender, add the *gabi* and radishes and cook until soft. Put in the *kangkong*, or mustard leaves, and *sili*. Season with salt. Serve hot.
Note: *Calamansi* juice may be added if the dish is not sour enough.

Embutido

Serves: 8

⅓ kilo ground pork
2 x 145 grams cans Vienna sausage
1 *chorizo de Bilbao*
⅓ cup raisins
½ cup chopped sweet pickles
4 eggs, beaten
½ cup grated Edam cheese (*queso de bola*)
1 teaspoon vet-sin (monosodium glutamate)
5 slices American bread, moistened with evaporated milk
salt and pepper to taste

Finely chop and grind pork, sausage and *chorizo*. Mix with all other ingredients. Season with salt and pepper.

Wrap in buttered aluminum foil and bake at 350ºF for 30 minutes. Open wrapper and continue baking until golden-brown.

Katsudon

(Japanese in origin)

Serves: 4

3 small pork chops, or 2 large pork chops
salt and pepper
flour
1 egg, beaten
breadcrumbs
lard for frying
2 cups packaged American variety rice, cooked

1 cup chicken broth
2 tablespoons Kikkoman soy sauce
1-2 tablespoons sugar
1 teaspoon vet-sin (monosodium glutamate)
1½ cups leeks, cut diagonally into 1½ inch slices (use only the white parts)
4 eggs

Trim off some of the fat from the pork chops. Season with salt and pepper. Dredge with flour, roll in the beaten egg, then roll in breadcrumbs. Fry until golden-brown. Remove bones and cut meat into 1 inch pieces. Place the rice in a ceramic Japanese soup bowl. Set aside.

Mix broth, soy sauce, sugar and vet-sin in a saucepan. When boiling, add pork and leeks. After the liquid boils a second time, strain it from the meat and leeks and pour it onto the rice. Beat the eggs slightly and add to the leeks and the pork chops. Put this on top of the rice, leave it to steam for a few minutes, then serve.

Pork and chicken adobo

Serves: 6

1 chicken (about 1 to 1¼ kilos)
½ kilo pork
¾ cup native vinegar
1 tablespoon black pepper
salt to taste
1 head garlic, pounded
½ cup (approx.) water
lard for frying
2 tablespoons soy sauce
3 chicken livers
2 tablespoons water

Cut chicken into serving pieces and the pork into 2 inch squares. Place in a saucepan and add vinegar, black pepper, salt and garlic. Let stand for about one hour. Remove chicken.

Boil and then simmer pork first in the mixture until almost tender. Add chicken and simmer. When this sauce mixture becomes dry add about ½ cup water. Simmer about 30 minutes or until meats are almost tender. Fish out the garlic from the *adobo* sauce and fry in a little lard. Remove pork and chicken from *adobo* sauce and brown. Add soy sauce and the *adobo* sauce to the meat. Continue cooking until tender. Pound the liver and combine it with 2 tablespoons of water. Add to the sauce to thicken. Simmer for about 5 minutes.

Carne rellenada

Serves: 6-8

Wrapping
½ kilo pork leg or shoulder, tapa cut
4 cloves garlic
salt and pepper

Filling
¼ kilo ground pork
1 x 8 oz (250g) can Vienna sausage, chopped (save 2 pieces)
1 chorizo de Bilbao, chopped
⅓ cup chopped sweet mixed pickles
⅓ cup grated Edam cheese (queso de bola)
1 tablespoon all-purpose flour
salt and pepper to taste
1 teaspoon vet-sin (monosodium glutamate)
2 eggs
2 hard boiled eggs, quartered
1 small carrot (cut into 3 inch by ½ inch strips)
1 cucumber pickle

Flavoring
1 medium-sized onion, sliced
1 medium-sized tomato, sliced
4 cloves garlic
½ bay leaf
1 teaspoon peppercorns
3 tablespoons cooking sherry
1½ cups chicken broth

Sauce
2 tablespoons butter
2 tablespoons flour, toasted
strained sauce of pork
salt, pepper and vet-sin (monosodium glutamate) to taste

Spread the pork meat open. Rub well with chopped garlic, salt, and pepper. Set aside.

Mix filling of ground pork, Vienna sausage, chorizo de Bilbao, pickles, cheese, salt and pepper, vet-sin, raw eggs and flour.

Place half of the filling in the middle of the pork. Arrange the two Vienna sausages (cut into halves lengthwise), the hard boiled eggs, the carrot and pickle on top of it. Cover with the rest of the filling and roll. Sew where meat overlaps. Wrap the whole in tin foil.

Place in a Dutch Oven and add flavoring ingredients — onion, tomato, garlic, bay leaf, peppercorns and sherry.

Bring to a boil, then add the chicken broth. Simmer until the pork is tender (about 1 hour). Remove the foil package, unwrap the meat roll and brown lightly in 2 tablespoons lard. Slice and arrange on a platter. Pour the sauce (see below) around the meat roll.

To make sauce
Melt the butter, add toasted flour and the strained sauce of the pork. Cook until thick and season with salt, pepper and vet-sin.

Lagat na puso

Serves: 6

1 banana heart (*butuan* variety)
1 tablespoon salt
½ cup finely cut pork
4 tablespoons lard
4 cloves garlic
1 medium-sized onion, sliced
½ cup shrimps, shelled
½ cup vinegar
salt and pepper to taste

Remove hard covering of banana heart (about three petals) and slice the inner softer sections with the banana blossoms, crosswise. Sprinkle banana sections and blossoms with salt and squeeze. Rinse and drain. Set aside.

Fry the pork in 1 tablespoon lard and set aside. Sauté the garlic in 3 tablespoons lard, add the onion, shrimps and vinegar. Boil until the shrimps are thoroughly cooked. Add the pork and continue cooking for 5 minutes. Put in the squeezed blossoms and cook until tender. Season with salt and pepper.

Pancit Canton

Serves: 8-10

½ kilo shrimps
2 slices ginger, crushed and soaked in 2 tablespoons water
½ kilo pork
1 chicken breast
1 egg white
2 tablespoons cornstarch
1 medium-sized onion, sliced
cooking oil
6 Chinese mushrooms
3 cups chicken broth
1 teaspoon vet-sin (monosodium glutamate)
salt and pepper to taste

1 cauliflower, washed, divided into flowerettes
10 *apulid*, sliced
¼ kilo *chicharo*
1 carrot, cut crosswise into ⅛ inch slices
½ cabbage
3 stems celery, cut into 1 inch pieces
3-4 dashes sesame oil
¾ kilo noodles
2 scrambled eggs (see below)
¼ cup thin strips of ham

Peel shrimps, reserving the tails. Slit back of shrimps and remove black veins. Add a little ginger juice and wash. Thinly slice pork and chicken into 1 inch squares. Add a little egg white and cornstarch.

Sauté onion in a little oil and add shrimps, cooking until fishy taste is removed. Add pork and chicken and cook thoroughly. Place mushrooms, broth, vet-sin, salt and pepper in pan.

When pork is tender, thicken with a little cornstarch diluted in water. Add vegetables and boil once. Sprinkle sesame oil. Set aside.

In another pan, boil a little water. Put in the noodles and cook just enough to soften. Wash in cold water. Arrange on a platter and pour the sauce over it. Make firm scrambled egg and slice into small pieces. Decorate *pancit canton* with egg and sliced ham.

Firm scrambled egg
Beat eggs slightly, season with salt and pepper to taste. Heat 1 teaspoon oil in pan. When hot, pour in egg mixture. Tilt pan to spread egg thinly. Turn over once.

Stuffed Fish Fillets (see recipe on page 26)

Planked Tenderloin with Sautéed Mushrooms (see recipe opposite)

Planked tenderloin with sautéed mushrooms

(See photograph opposite)

Serves: 8

6 tablespoons butter
3 tablespoons chopped red bell pepper
3 tablespoons chopped green bell pepper
3 tablespoons chopped onion
1 tablespoon chopped parsley
1 tablespoon chopped garlic

salt and pepper
1 tablespoon lemon juice
½ cup sliced mushrooms
2 tablespoons butter for frying
8 pieces tenderloin (about 1 kilo)
¾ to 1 inch thick
mashed potatoes (see below)

Cream butter. Add the red and green pepper, onion, parsley, garlic, salt, pepper and lemon juice. Set aside. Sauté mushrooms in a small amount of butter. Set aside.

In an iron skillet, fry tenderloin quickly in hot butter. Spread half of the butter mixture on the bottom of a Pyrex platter. Arrange meat, then spread the rest of the mixture on top. Sprinkle with sautéed mushrooms. Decorate rim of oval platter with mashed potatoes. Broil until potatoes are golden-brown.

Mashed potatoes
¾ kilo potatoes
2 egg yolks (raw)
4 tablespoons butter
½ cup milk
salt, pepper and vet-sin (monosodium glutamate)

Boil the potatoes. Peel and mash them. Add egg yolk, butter, and milk. Season with salt, pepper and vet-sin. Beat well.

Pastel de pollo

Serves: 12-15

1 chicken (about 1 kilo)
salt and pepper
lard
4 tablespoons butter
1 medium-sized onion, chopped
1 x 4 oz (125 grams) can champignon mushrooms, cut in halves
1 x 145 grams can Vienna sausage, sliced
I piece *chorizo de Bilbao* (El Rey or local equivalent), thinly sliced
2 cups chicken broth
3 tablespoons sherry
2 small carrots, peeled and cubed

4 medium-sized potatoes, peeled and cubed
¾ to 1 cup grated Edam cheese (*queso de bola*)
salt and pepper
½ teaspoon vet-sin (monosodium glutamate)
flour
water
½ cup olives
1 pie crust (see below)
1 egg yolk
melted butter

Cut the chicken into serving pieces. Sprinkle with salt and pepper and brown slightly in lard. Remove chicken.

Melt the butter and cook onion until soft. Add the mushrooms and the Vienna sausage and cook for about 3 minutes. Add the chicken pieces and the Spanish sausage and cook for another 3 minutes. Pour in broth and sherry. Simmer for 30 minutes or until the chicken is tender. Add carrots, potatoes and grated cheese. Continue cooking until the carrots are tender. Season with salt, pepper and vet-sin. Thicken with a little flour diluted in a small quantity of water.

Pour mixture in a pyrex dish and arrange olives on top. Cover with pie crust (see below) and brush with a mixture of egg yolk and butter. Make small x-cuts on the crust. Strips of flattened pastry may be used to decorate top. Bake at 400°F for 20 minutes or until golden-brown.

Pie crust
1½ cups all-purpose flour
8 tablespoons Crisco shortening (Dari-creme or margarine)
½ teaspoon salt
4 tablespoons cold water

Add shortening and salt to flour and cut with a pastry blender until well blended. Add enough water to form into a ball. Roll out dough. Use to cover the *pastel*.

Kue Kiam

Serves: 6

¼ kilo pork fat, cut into fine pieces
meat of 1 *bid-bid* (about ⅓ kilo), or
2 *dalagang bukid*, mashed
½ kilo shrimps, chopped
4 eggs
⅓ cup cornstarch
1 teaspoon vet-sin (monosodium glutamate)
salt and pepper to taste
some chopped spring onions
¼ kilo leaf lard
2 eggs, beaten
lard for frying

Mix all ingredients together and wrap in leaf lard with ends tucked in to form a 3 by 6 inch long sausage. Steam this sausage for 30 minutes. Remove from steamer and cool. Cut into ⅓ inch slices diagonally and dip in beaten egg. Fry in lard until golden-brown. Serve with sweet and sour radish.

Sweet and Sour Radish
4-5 radishes
2 tablespoons salt for each sprinkling
⅓ cup sugar
3 tablespoons cider vinegar

Peel and slice radishes very thinly. Add salt. Squeeze radishes and rinse in water. Repeat 3 times. Marinate with sugar, and vinegar for about 3 minutes.

Chicken relleno

Serves: 12

1 large chicken (about 1½ kilos)
1 tablespoon *calamansi*, or lemon
juice
3 tablespoons soy sauce

Stuffing

5 slices American bread, soaked in
evaporated milk
½ kilo pork meat
1 x 8 oz (250 grams) can *chorizo de
Bilbao* (4-5 pieces), or 1 *chorizo* El
Rey brand
2 x 145 grams cans Vienna sausage
½ cup chopped pineapple
10 green olives, chopped

5 eggs, beaten
⅓ cup raisins
⅔ cup chopped sweet pickles
½ cup grated Edam cheese (*queso
de bola*)
salt and pepper to taste
1 teaspoon vet-sin (monosodium
glutamate)
butter for cooking

Slit the back of the chicken with a sharp knife. Carefully remove all bones, leaving
the meat and skin intact. Remove the big bones of the wings and legs, leaving
only the small wing bones and the end of the drumstick. Soak the chicken in
calamansi, or lemon juice, and soy sauce for 30 minutes. Then stuff bird as
follows.

To make stuffing

Soak the American bread in evaporated milk. Set aside.

Grind the pork. Chop the *chorizo de Bilbao*, Vienna sausage, pineapple, olives
and slices of moistened American bread. Combine all these ingredients. Add the
eggs, raisins, pickles and cheese. Season with salt, pepper and vet-sin.

Fill the boneless chicken with the stuffing and sew the slit at the back. Wrap
chicken with buttered aluminum foil and press the leg parts of the stuffed
chicken to make it even. Place the stuffed chicken in a baking dish. Bake at
350°F for 1 hour. Remove the buttered aluminium foil wrapper and continue
baking until chicken is golden-brown.

Pastel de lengua

Serves: 12-15

4 tablespoons butter
1 medium-sized onion, chopped
1 x 4 oz (125 grams) can champignon mushrooms, cut into halves
1 x 8 oz (250 grams) can Vienna sausage, cut crosswise (4 cuts per piece)
1½ kilos cooked ox tongue, cut into ¾ inch cubes
liquid in which ox tongue was boiled
3 tablespoons sherry
½ cup grated Edam cheese (*queso de bola*)
1 teaspoon vet-sin (monosodium glutamate)
2 carrots, peeled and cut into 1 inch cubes
4 potatoes, peeled and cut into 1 inch cubes
a little flour dissolved in water
½ cup green olives
1 pie crust (see below)
1 egg yolk
2 tablespoons butter

Heat butter in a pan and sauté the onions for about 3 minutes. Add mushrooms and Vienna sausage and cook about 2 minutes. Put in the tongue. Strain the liquid in which the tongue was boiled and pour it in. When boiling, add sherry, cheese, vet-sin, carrots and potatoes. Cook until potatoes are tender. Thicken sauce with a little flour dissolved in water.

Pour into a Pyrex dish and top with olives. Cover with pie crust and brush with egg yolk mixed with butter. Prick crust and bake at 400ºF for 20 minutes or until golden-brown.

Pie crust
1½ cups all-purpose flour
8 tablespoons Crisco shortening
½ teaspoon salt
4 tablespoons cold water

Add shortening to flour and cut with a pastry blender until well blended. Add enough water to form into a ball. Roll out dough and use to cover the *pastel*.

Chicken palmer

Serves: 4

1 chicken (1 kilo)
salt and pepper
3 tablespoons flour
lard for frying
1 medium-sized onion, chopped
½ teaspoon curry powder

½ tablespoon sugar
2 cups rice for serving
1 cup water
1 x 245 grams can whole tomatoes
½ cup milk
1 tablespoon flour

Cut the chicken into serving pieces. Dredge with salt, pepper and flour and brown in hot lard. Remove the chicken and add a little more lard to the pan.

Sauté the chopped onion until soft. Remove from heat and add the curry powder, sugar and flour. Add water and stir over the heat until thick. Add tomatoes, the chicken, salt and pepper. Simmer 30 minutes or until tender. Add milk and cook 10 minutes. Serve with a border of rice. (Grease a ring mould with butter. Press tightly about 2 cups cooked rice in mould. Unmould, by inverting into round platter. Put chicken in middle, and around the sides.)

Timbal de macarrones

(See photograph on page 63)

Serves: 10

1 box Muellers egg noodles (or see noodles recipe opposite)
4 tablespoons butter
1 small size onion, chopped
¼ kilo cooked ham, chopped
½ chicken (about 1 kilo), boiled
1 x 2 oz (60g) can pâté de foie gras
1 cup chicken broth
3 tablespoons sherry
Béchamel sauce (see opposite)

½ cup grated Edam cheese (*queso de bola*)
salt and pepper to taste
1 teaspoon vet-sin (monosodium glutamate)
4 eggs
6-7 spring onion stems, for decoration
1 piece *pimento*, cut into ½ inch slices, for decoration

Boil the noodles in salted water until tender. Wash and let stand in cold water. Set aside. Drain when ready for use.

Melt and heat butter in a pan. Cook onion until soft. Add ham, chicken, and pâté de foie gras and cook for 3 minutes. Add broth, noodles, sherry, half the Béchamel sauce, and grated cheese. Season with salt, pepper and vet-sin. Cook for 3 minutes. Remove from the heat and let cool. When slightly cool add the lightly beaten eggs.

Pour the noodle mixture into a greased loaf pan. Stand this pan in another pan of hot water and bake at 375ºF for about 30 minutes, or until firm. Turn out onto a serving platter and cover with other half of Béchamel sauce. Decorate with spring onions and *pimento* slices.

Béchamel sauce

2 tablespoons butter
3 level tablespoons all-purpose flour
1 cup chicken broth
½ cup milk
salt and cayenne or white pepper to taste

Melt butter in pan. Remove from heat. Stir in flour and broth. Return to stove and cook at a low heat until slightly thick. Add milk. Cook some more, stirring, until thick. Season with salt and pepper to taste.

Noodles

1 ¼ cup all-purpose flour
½ teaspoon salt
2 egg yolks
generous amount of cornstarch
2 tablespoons cooking oil

Place flour on a slab or flat surface. Make a well in the center and pour in salt and egg yolks. Work to a smooth paste with water. Knead mixture, sprinkling generously with cornstarch to prevent stickiness.

When rolled out smoothly to ⅛ inch thick, roll up into a dough-like sausage. Cut crosswise into ⅛ inch thick strips. Unroll strips. Boil in water seasoned with a little salt to taste, and oil. Wash in cold water. Drain when ready for use.

Kare-kareng buntot

Serves: 6

1 oxtail (1½ to 2 kilos)
5 tablespoons lard
5 cloves garlic, crushed
1 medium-sized onion, sliced
water of ¼ cup achuete, soaked
1 banana heart, sliced crosswise
2 bundles stringbeans, cut in 2 inch lengths

4 eggplants, cut in ½ inch slices
⅓ cup rice, ground to a powder and toasted in a pan
½ cup peanut butter
salt and pepper
1 teaspoon vet-sin (monosodium glutamate)

Clean the oxtail and cut into 3 inch pieces. Boil once and discard water. Boil again until tender.

In lard, sauté garlic and onion. Add achuete water and meat and bring to a boil. Add vegetables and enough broth to make a sauce. Add the powdered rice, and peanut butter dissolved in ¾ cup water. Season with salt, pepper and vet-sin to taste. Serve with binagoongan.

Binagoongan
3 tablespoons lard
4 cloves garlic, crushed
1 small onion, sliced
½ cup pork, cooked and sliced
¼ inch x 1 inch
2 tablespoons achuete water
1 cup bagoong
2 tablespoons vinegar
1 tablespoon sugar

Sauté garlic and onion in lard. Add pork, achuete water and bagoong. Add vinegar and sugar. Bring to a boil for a few minutes.

Timbal de Macarrones (see recipe on page 60)

Tongue with Mushroom Sauce (see recipe on page 79)

Cannelloni al Italianne (see recipe on page 82)

Tomato and Crab Salad (see recipe on page 90)

Saté Babi

Serves: 10

1 kilo pork tenderloin
6 tablespoons *calamansi* juice
⅔ cup brown sugar
8 tablespoons soy sauce
4 tablespoons rum
1 teaspoon vet-sin (monosodium glutamate)
1 head garlic, crushed
½ cup Mafran sauce

Cut pork tenderloin into 1 inch pieces. Marinate with the *calamansi* juice, brown sugar, soy sauce, rum, vet-sin and garlic for at least 3 hours.

Before cooking drain and arrange on skewers, 4 to 5 pieces on each. Roast on live coals. Add Mafran sauce to the marinade. When meat is cooked, brush with the marinade and roast a further 2 minutes.

Serve with saté sauce.

Saté Sauce

3 tablespoons peanut butter
½ cup water
4 tablespoons soy sauce
3 tablespoons *calamansi* juice
3½ tablespoons sugar
6 cloves garlic, pounded
1 small onion, sliced
1 chili pepper, sliced
1 teaspoon butter
2 tablespoons chopped peanuts
salt and pepper

Dilute peanut butter with water. Add soy sauce, *calamansi* juice and sugar. Set aside. In a mortar pound garlic, sliced onion and chilli pepper. Combine with the peanut butter mixture, then strain. Cook over low heat until mixture boils. Remove from heat and stir in butter, peanuts, salt and pepper.

Roast squab chicken

Serves: 4

4 spring chickens (½ kilo each)

Stuffing
½ loaf American bread (8 slices)
1 cup finely cut uncooked bacon
1 tablespoon chopped parsley
2 tablespoons butter
dash of thyme
dash of sage
1 cup finely cut celery
1 small onion, chopped
4 eggs
salt and pepper to taste

Flavoring
salt, pepper and paprika to season
2 tablespoons butter
4 slices raw bacon, 3 inches long
1 medium-sized onion, sliced
1 small carrot, pared and sliced
thinly crosswise
1 stem celery, sliced
1 small bay leaf
½ head garlic, crushed
3 tablespoons cooking sherry
¼ cup salad oil

Sauce
1½ cups chicken stock
2 tablespoons butter
½ cup all-purpose flour
salt, pepper and vet-sin
(monosodium glutamate) to taste

Clean and season the chickens with salt and pepper. Mix all stuffing ingredients and stuff the chickens. Sew up the opening of each chicken. With a piece of string tie the legs to the tail, then with another string, tie the wings together at the back.

Place chicken squabs in a shallow pan, sprinkle with salt, pepper and paprika. Put one bacon slice and ½ tablespoon butter on each chicken. Arrange the vegetables around the birds and pour sherry and salad oil on the chickens. Bake at 350°F for about one hour, or until chickens are tender. Remove chicken from pan and arrange on serving dishes.

To make sauce

To the drippings and the vegetables, add chicken stock and stir until well mixed. Strain. Set aside.

In a saucepan melt butter and add flour. Blend for three minutes. Remove from heat and add the strained liquid, previously set aside, to the butter-flour mixture. Return pan to heat and stir, season with salt, pepper and vet-sin.

Pour sauce over chicken and serve.

Tapa

Serves: 10

6 tablespoons sugar
4 tablespoons salt
½ teaspoon vet-sin (monosodium glutamate)
¼ teaspoon saltpeter
1 kilo beef sirloin, or pork shoulder (kasim) preferably without fat, thinly sliced into 3 x 5 inch pieces
¾ cup pineapple juice

Combine sugar, salt, vet-sin and saltpeter. Put a little of the mixture on each slice of meat and rub in well. Arrange meat pieces one on top of the other, and pour pineapple juice over it. Keep in the refrigerator for 2 days. Fry in a little lard before serving.

Cueta

Serves: 6

¼ kilo ground pork
1 kilo chicken meat, chopped
10 *apulid*, chopped
4 Chinese mushrooms, chopped
1 small onion
½-⅔ cup *labong*
3 egg yolks
3 tablespoons soy sauce

salt and pepper
2 tablespoons cornstarch
½ teaspoon *Ngo Yong* powder
· *untosinsal*, or leaf lard
2 egg whites
¼ cup water
¾ cup cornstarch
½ teaspoon salt

Mix pork, chicken, *apulid*, mushrooms, onion and *labong*. Add the egg yolks, soy sauce, salt, pepper and cornstarch. Put in *Ngo Yong*. Wrap in *untosinsal* like a fat sausage. Immerse in a batter made of egg white, water, cornstarch and salt. Fry in deep fat and slice. Serve with radish in sweet and sour sauce (see page 57).

Chicken à la King

Serves: 8

3 tablespoons butter
1 medium-sized onion, chopped
½ cup diced champignon mushrooms
1 kilo chicken, cooked and diced
2 pieces *pimento*, diced
white sauce (see **opposite**)
1 large loaf American bread (16 slices)
butter for spreading
parsley sprigs

Melt butter in a pan. Sauté onion for about 2 minutes, then add mushrooms, chicken, *pimento* and white sauce (see below).

Remove the crust of American bread and spread slices with butter. Mould bread in muffin pan and toast. Fill with Chicken à la King and decorate with sprigs of parsley.

White sauce
2 tablespoons butter
3 tablespoons flour
1 cup chicken broth
½ cup milk

Melt the butter in a pan. Remove from heat and stir in flour and broth. Return to heat and stir until thick, then blend in milk to make a smooth sauce.

Dinuguan

Serves: 6

½ kilo pork shoulder (*kasim*), or ham (*pique*) diced into ½ inch squares
²/₃ cup native vinegar
1 large onion, sliced
½ teaspoon crushed peppercorns
salt
3 tablespoons lard
6 cloves garlic, pounded

½ cup pork blood
2 cups water
2 sprigs oregano
1 teaspoon vet-sin (monosodium glutamate)
2 teaspoons sugar
2 tablespoons *patis*
2 large hot peppers (not *labuyo*)

Soak pork in vinegar with onion, pepper and salt. Set aside.

Sauté garlic in lard, put in marinated pork and bring to a boil. Cover and simmer for 30 minutes until pork is tender and the sauce is almost dry. Chop coagulated pork blood and add. Blend well. Add water, oregano, vet-sin, sugar and *patis*. Drop in hot peppers and simmer for 10 minutes.

Humba

Serves: 6

1 kilo pork, cut into 2 inch pieces
2 onions, cut into 6 or 8 pieces
2 tablespoons sugar
¾ cup water
4 tablespoons soy sauce

Combine all the ingredients. Simmer until the meat is tender.

Paella à la Valenciana

(See photograph on cover)

Serves: 12-15

½ kilo pork tenderloin
1 chicken (a little less than 1 kilo)
½ kilo large shrimps
salt and pepper
½ cup olive oil
3 large crabs
2 cups clams (halaan)
½ teaspoon paprika
4 cloves garlic, chopped
1 medium-sized onion, chopped
1 green bell pepper, sliced into
1 inch pieces
2 chorizo de Bilbao, sliced thinly

3 cups packaged rice (American variety)
½ cup tomato sauce
6 cups clam broth
1 small bay leaf
salt, pepper and vet-sin for seasoning
¼ teaspoon saffron, mixed with
1 tablespoon water (optional)
1 cup frozen peas
2 pieces pimento, cut into 1 inch squares
2 hard boiled eggs

Cut pork and chicken into 1½ inch pieces. Brown in oil. Shell shrimps leaving tail. Slit shrimps at the back and remove black veins. Wash shrimps and dredge with salt and pepper. Brown in oil and set aside.

Boil crabs and quarter. Crack shells of crab claws. Boil clams and remove the empty top shells.

Heat olive oil in a pan and add chicken, pork, paprika, garlic, onion, pepper and *chorizo*. Toss for a few minutes and add unwashed rice and stir until the rice is slightly brown. Add tomato sauce, broth, bay leaf, salt, pepper and vet-sin. Add shrimps. Bring to a boil. Add saffron and water. Transfer to a serving casserole and bake at 350ºF for 30 minutes.

Uncover the casserole and arrange clams, crabs, frozen peas and *pimento* on top. Cover and cook for 5 minutes. Serve decorated with slices of hard boiled eggs.

Chicken croquettes

Serves: 6

1 chicken (1 kilo), boiled (save broth for white sauce)
white sauce (see below)
salt and pepper
1 teaspoon vet-sin
  (monosodium glutamate)

flour
2 eggs, beaten
1 cup breadcrumbs
lard for frying

Chop chicken meat and mix with white sauce (see below). Season with salt, pepper and vet-sin and place in freezer to harden. When mixture is firm, form into croquettes, the size of quail eggs. Roll in flour, then beaten eggs, and finally in breadcrumbs. Fry in deep fat until golden-brown.

White sauce
2 tablespoons butter
3 tablespoons all-purpose flour
salt
cayenne pepper
1 cup chicken broth
½ cup milk

Melt butter in a pan. Remove from heat and add flour, salt, and cayenne pepper and broth. Cook over low heat, stirring constantly until thick. Blend in milk and combine to stir and cook until sauce is thick.

Sweet and sour pork

Serves: 4-5

½ kilo pork tenderloin
3 tablespoons native vinegar
3 tablespoons soy sauce
2 tablespoons sugar
½ head garlic, crushed
1 egg
½ cup cornstarch
½ cup flour
cornstarch for rolling
lard for deep frying
salt and pepper

Cut pork into 1 inch pieces. Marinate in mixture of vinegar, soy sauce, sugar and garlic for 1½ hours. Drain meat. Mix together egg, cornstarch and flour. Roll each piece of pork in cornstarch mixture and deep fry.

Sauce

2 tablespoons cider vinegar
6 tablespoons sugar
1 cup water
3 tablespoons catsup
1 teaspoon oyster sauce
½ teaspoon salt
2 tablespoons cornstarch, diluted with 2-3 tablespoons water
2 tomatoes, cut into wedges
2 medium-sized onions, cut into 8 pieces

1 carrot, sliced in rounds
2 stems celery, cut into 1 inch pieces
½ cup pineapple tidbits
¼ cup chopped green bell pepper, cut into 1 x 1 inch pieces
¼ cup chopped red bell pepper, cut into 1 x 1 inch pieces

Combine the first 6 ingredients in a frying pan. Thicken with cornstarch mixture. Add tomatoes, onions, carrot, celery, pineapple, and red and green bell peppers. Boil once, add pork and serve hot.

Chicken Salad (see recipe on page 89)

Vegetable Salad (see recipe on page 90)

Calderetta

Serves: 8

2 kilos goat meat, cut into 2 inch pieces
¾ cup native vinegar
1 head garlic, crushed
salt and freshly ground pepper to taste
¼ cup cooking oil
3 large onions, sliced
¼ cup sherry
½ cup olive oil
1 small bay leaf
1 sprig parsley
1 teaspoon whole peppercorns
6 cloves garlic

1 hot green pepper
½ cup tomato sauce
2 cups warm water
a slice of goat liver (about 5 inches square, ½ inch thick)
½ cup water
1 x 200 grams can *pimento*
½ cup grated Edam cheese (*queso de bola*)
1 teaspoon vet-sin (monosodium glutamate)
1 teaspoon sugar
1 cup green olives

One day before marinate goat meat in a mixture of vinegar, garlic, pepper and salt.

The next day drain the meat and brown little by little in hot oil. Place browned meat in a saucepan and add onions and sherry. Bring to a boil, then add olive oil and bay leaf.

In a mortar crush parsley, peppercorns, garlic and pepper. Add them to mixture in saucepan and then put in tomato sauce and water. Simmer until goat meat is tender.

Brown a slice of goat liver in hot lard then pound into a paste. Add water to the pounded liver and strain. Add the liver paste to the meat, stirring continuously until it boils. Add the *pimento* and the grated cheese. Season with vet-sin and sugar to taste. Add olives and serve.

Pompadour Milanaise

(Beehive Macaroni)

Serves: 15

⅔ of 1 x 454 **grams package Royal** macaroni
4 tablespoons butter
1 medium-sized onion, chopped
1 x 8 oz (250 g) can mushrooms, diced finely
1 x 8 oz (250g) can Vienna sausage, diced finely
¾ cup tomato sauce
1 cup chicken broth

1 x 4 oz (125 g) can pâté de foie gras
¼ kilo ham, diced finely
3 tablespoons cooking sherry
1 cup grated Edam cheese (*queso de bola*)
1 teaspoon vet-sin (monosodium glutamate)
salt and pepper to taste
6 eggs

Boil the macaroni in salted water until soft. Wash in cold water. Cut into ⅓ inch pieces. Line a well-greased 9 inch aluminum mixing bowl with enough noodles to cover the bowl, putting the noodle pieces together side by side with the holes showing.

Melt the butter in a pan. Add the onion and cook until transparent. Add the mushrooms and Vienna sausage and cook for 5 minutes. Put in the tomato sauce and chicken broth. Simmer until mixture thickens, then add the pâté de foie gras and the ham. Put in the rest of the macaroni, sherry, and grated cheese. Add vet-sin, salt and pepper to season. Cook for 2 minutes more, then remove from heat. Mix in slightly beaten eggs and fill macaroni-lined mould.

Put bowl in another pan of hot water and bake at 350ºF for about 30 minutes, or until brown. Cool slightly. Loosen macaroni beehive with spatula. Turn over onto a round platter.

Pour a little tomato sauce (see below) on the top and the rest around the sides so beehive holes are visible.

Tomato sauce
2 tablespoons butter
1 teaspoon chopped garlic
1 tablespoon all-purpose flour
2 tablespoons tomato paste **or**
    ⅓ cup tomato sauce
1 cup water
4 tablespoons grated Edam cheese
(*queso de bola*)
salt and pepper to taste

Melt butter in a pan, add the garlic and the flour. Cook for 2 minutes then put in the tomato paste or sauce and the broth. Simmer until thick, then add the cheese, salt and pepper.

Tongue with mushroom sauce

(See photograph on page 64)

Serves: 8

1 ox tongue
salt
vinegar
cooking oil for browning the tongue
6 cloves garlic, crushed
1 medium-sized onion, sliced
2 medium-sized tomatoes, sliced
3 tablespoons olive oil
1 small bay leaf
1 clove (*clavos de comer*)
salt and peppercorns
1 tablespoon soy sauce

3 tablespoons sherry
3 cups water
1 x 4 oz (125 g) can champignon mushrooms, sliced crosswise into 3 to 4 pieces
3 tablespoons butter
2 tablespoons flour
4 tablespoons grated Edam cheese (*queso de bola*)
1 teaspoon vet-sin (monosodium glutamate)

Rub the tongue with salt and vinegar. Blanch the tongue in boiling water and scrape off the white coating. Prick with fork to allow flavor of other ingredients to penetrate. Brown in oil.

Sauté garlic, onion and tomatoes in olive oil. Cook 3 minutes. Add the tongue, bay leaf, clove, salt and peppercorns, soy sauce, sherry, and water. Simmer for 3 hours or until tongue is tender. Remove tongue and slice it. Strain cooking liquid and set aside.

In another pan sauté mushrooms in one tablespoon butter. Set aside. Melt the rest of the butter and add the flour. Stir for 2 minutes then remove from heat.

Return strained cooking liquid from the tongue to the heat. Gradually add butter and flour mixture and cook until slightly thick. Add the sliced tongue, sautéed mushrooms, and grated cheese. Season with salt and vet-sin to taste. Arrange the tongue in a chafing dish and pour remaining sauce over it.

Lumpiang Shanghai

Serves: 6

½ kilo ground pork
¼ kilo shrimps, chopped
¼ cup chopped dried Chinese mushrooms
½ cup chopped *apulid*, or *singkamas*
¼ cup chopped spring onions

2 egg yolks
3 tablespoons soy sauce
1 teaspoon vet-sin (monosodium glutamate)
3 dashes of sesame oil
salt and pepper
sweet and sour sauce (see below)

Combine pork, shrimps, mushrooms, *apulid* or *singkamas*, spring onions, egg yolks, soy sauce, vet-sin, sesame oil, salt and pepper. Wrap into thin rolls in *lumpia* wrapper and fry in deep fat. Cut into 1½ inch pieces. Serve with sweet and sour sauce.

Sweet and sour sauce

2 tablespoons cider vinegar
1 cup water
6 tablespoons sugar
½ teaspoon salt
1 tablespoon catsup

1 teaspoon oyster sauce
1 heaped tablespoon cornstarch
3 tablespoons water, for dissolving cornstarch

Mix vinegar, water, sugar and salt in a saucepan, then add catsup and oyster sauce. Bring to the boil.

Dissolve cornstarch in water and add to the boiling mixture stirring vigorously until thick.

Roast turkey

Serves: 30

1 turkey (about 19 lbs or 8.6 kilos)
6 tablespoons soy sauce
1 tablespoon lemon juice
2 cloves garlic

Stuffing

5 slices American bread, soaked in evaporated milk
½ kilo pork meat
1 x 8 oz (250 grams) can Purefoods *chorizo de Bilbao* (4 pieces), or
1 *chorizo* El Rey brand
2 x 145 grams cans Vienna sausage
10 small green olives, chopped
5 eggs
²/₃ cup chopped sweet pickles
⅓ cup raisins
½ cup grated Edam cheese (*queso de bola*)
salt and pepper to taste
1 teaspoon vet-sin (monosodium glutamate)
lard for roasting turkey
3 tablespoons sherry (optional)

The day before cooking, soak the turkey in soy sauce and lemon juice. The following day rub well with garlic and then stuff turkey as follows.

To make stuffing

Soak the American bread in evaporated milk. Set aside.

Chop the pork meat, *chorizo de Bilbao*, Vienna sausage, olives and moistened American bread. Combine all these ingredients. Add eggs, pickles, raisins and cheese. Mix thoroughly. Season with salt, pepper and vet-sin.

Stuff the turkey with the mixture through the neck. Leave skin on chest intact and sew the opening. Tie turkey legs together, leaving a 2 inch gap between. Connect legs with string to the tail end. Press the wings against the sides of the body securing joints by tying them with a string passing over the back.

Brush all the meat surface with lard and place turkey in a roasting pan. Arrange ¼ inch slices of pork skin, or solid lard, on the bird to prevent the skin from drying out and pour sherry over it. Roast the bird at 300ºF for 3 hours, or until tender, and baste frequently during cooking.

Gravy

neck, gizzard, liver of turkey
2 tablespoons butter
2 tablespoons toasted flour
salt, pepper
1 teaspoon vet-sin (monosodium glutamate)
¼ cup (approx.) grated cheese

Boil the neck, gizzard and liver of the turkey for broth. Strain the broth and add to the turkey's drippings.

Melt butter in a pan. Remove from heat. Add toasted flour. Put in the turkey drippings mixed with 3 cups broth. Season with salt, pepper, vet-sin and a little grated cheese. Chop the cooked liver and add to the gravy. Cook for 5 minutes, or until gravy is thick.

Serve with mashed potato, cranberry sauce, gravy, celery and black olives.

Cannelloni al Italianne

(See photograph on page 65)

Serves: 12-15

Paste
1 cup all-purpose flour
½ teaspoon salt
3 egg yolks
generous amount of cornstarch for
sprinkling
2 tablespoons cooking oil

Filling
4 chicken livers
lard
½ cow brain
4 tablespoons butter
1 medium-sized onion, chopped
½ cup tomato sauce
½ kilo pork tenderloin, chopped
¼ kilo ham, chopped

1 x 2 oz (60 grams) can pâté de foie
gras, or liverwurst
½ teaspoon vet-sin
salt and pepper to taste
½ cup milk
3 tablespoons sherry
2 egg yolks

Place flour on a slab or a flat surface. Make a well in the center and pour in salt and egg yolks. Work it up to a smooth paste with a little water. Knead the dough until smooth. Roll out thinly and cut into 2 inch squares. Boil in hot water seasoned with salt and oil until tender. Wash and drain in cold water when ready for use.

Sauté chicken livers in lard and set aside. Blanch cow brain in boiling water to remove the membrane. Chop cow brain and sautéed chicken livers. Set aside.

In another pan, melt butter and cook onion until soft. Add tomato sauce and cook for 3 minutes. Add pork tenderloin, ham, pâté de foie gras, chopped liver and brain. Season with salt, pepper, and vet-sin and bring to a boil. Cook 3 minutes. Blend in milk and sherry. Remove from heat and add egg yolks.

Sauce
3 tablespoons butter
5 level tablespoons all-purpose flour
1½ cups milk
2 egg yolks, diluted in
2 tablespoons milk

Melt butter in pan. Remove from heat. Stir in flour and milk. Return to fire (slow), stir until slightly thick. Add egg yolks. Cook until thick, stirring over low heat.

To make up cannelloni
paste, filling and sauce (see opposite)
½ cup grated Edam cheese (*queso de bola*)
butter

Spread each piece of paste carefully onto a plate. Put a tablespoon of filling onto each and roll up. Arrange the cannelloni pieces on the bottom of a Pyrex dish and cover with a little sauce. Arrange another layer over the bottom one and cover with remaining sauce. Sprinkle with grated cheese, dot with butter and broil until golden-brown.

Pampango kilawin

Serves: 4

½ kilo pork, cut into ½ inch squares, as thinly as possible
¾ cup native vinegar
2 medium-sized onions, sliced
salt and crushed peppercorns
2 tablespoons lard
6 cloves garlic, crushed

¼ kilo pork liver, sliced into 1 inch squares
¾ cup water
salt and pepper
1 teaspoon vet-sin (monosodium glutamate)

Soak pork in ½ cup vinegar, one of the sliced onions, salt and crushed peppercorns.
Soak the liver in ¼ cup vinegar and add the other sliced onion, salt and peppercorns.
Sauté the garlic in lard. Add the pork and allow to boil. After it has boiled press pork hard against the pan with a kitchen spoon. Then cook until vinegar has evaporated. Add the liver and bring to a boil. Again, press against pan. Add water. Season with salt, pepper, and vet-sin.
Note: This dish is best served the following day.

Lumpiang Macao or siomai

Serves: 8

Wrapper
1 cup all-purpose flour
1 egg white
4 tablespoons lard
3 tablespoons water

Place flour on a wooden slab or flat surface. Make a well in the center and put in egg white, lard and water. Mix the ingredients in the center thoroughly, and quickly work in the flour. Knead well. Roll out thinly and cut into rounds 4 inches in diameter. Put filling in each wrapper.

Filling
½ kilo ground pork
¼ kilo shrimps, chopped
1 kilo cooked crabs (*alimasag*), shelled and chopped
3 tablespoons cornstarch
1 teaspoon vet-sin (monosodium glutamate)
3 tablespoons soy sauce
2 dashes sesame oil
3 tablespoons chopped spring onions
salt and pepper
6 Chinese mushrooms, soaked in water and chopped
10 *apulid*, or 1 small *singkamas*
2 eggs

Combine all the filling ingredients and place 1 heaped tablespoon in the center of each wrapper. Press wrapper up and around all sides of the *siomai*, leaving the center open. Arrange the filled wrappers in a steamer and steam for 15 minutes.

Serve with *calamansi* and *toyo*.

Vegetables and Salads

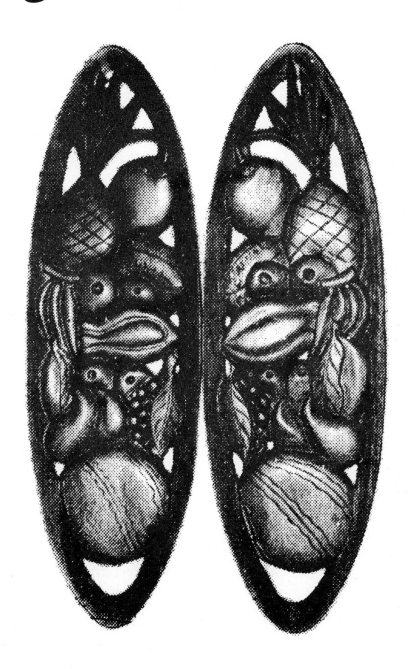

Lumpiang ubod

Serves: 10

2 kilos *ubod* (coconut heart)
1 clove garlic, crushed
1 medium-sized onion, chopped
lard for sautéeing
3 tablespoons *patis* (thin sauce)
½ kilo shrimps, shelled and sliced
(one shrimp may be cut in 2-3
pieces)

½ kilo boiled pork, sliced into
⅛ x ⅛ x 1 inch strips
1 kilo *alimasag* boiled, shelled, and
flaked
vet-sin (monosodium glutamate)
salt and pepper to taste
3 bunches native lettuce
lumpia wrappers (see below)

Slice *ubod* in shoestring fashion. Boil and drain.

In a pan, sauté garlic and onion in a little lard. Add *patis*, and shrimps and cook until fishy taste is removed. Add the pork and *alimasag* and bring to a boil. Season with salt and pepper and vet-sin. Put in the *ubod* and cook until tender. Wrap *ubod* mixture in *lumpia* wrapper with a piece of lettuce inside. Serve with sauce (see opposite).

Lumpia wrapper
Makes: 12 wrappers

2 eggs
2 tablespoons vegetable cooking oil,
or pork fat
1 cup cornstarch
1½ cups water
½ teaspoon salt
½ teaspoon vet-sin (monosodium
glutamate)

Beat eggs until thick and add oil. Beat in and add alternately cornstarch and water. Season with salt and vet-sin.

Heat oil in omelet pan before using to prevent sticking. When hot line bottom of pan with a thin coating of batter and cook until wrapper can be easily lifted. Tilt the pan to spread evenly.

Note: Make three recipes of *lumpia* wrapper to wrap *ubod* mixture above.

Sauce
1 cup sugar
3 cups water
3 tablespoons soy sauce
3 heaped tablespoons cornstarch
1½ teaspoons salt

Melt sugar in a saucepan over a low fire. In a bowl, mix a little water, soy sauce, cornstarch and salt into a smooth paste. Then add all the water to this paste. Pour this mixture into the melted sugar. Stir over heat until thick.

Pinakbet

Serves: 6

12 small eggplants, quartered and cut into 2 inch pieces
5 small *ampalaya*, quartered and cut into 2 inch pieces
6 *okra*, cut into 2 inch pieces
small bunch of *sitaw*, cut into 2 inch pieces
4 ripe tomatoes, chopped
4 slices of ginger, finely sliced
2 cups pork *sitsaron*, cut into 1½ inch pieces

⅓ cup fish *bagoong* (from Ilocos), or *alamang*
1 medium-sized onion, sliced
¼ cup tomato sauce
1½ cups water
6 cloves garlic, crushed
1 teaspoon vet-sin (monosodium glutamate)
2 tablespoons lard, or cooking oil

Boil eggplants, *ampalaya, okra, sitaw*, tomatoes, ginger, *sitsaron, bagoong*, onion and tomato sauce, in water. Do not stir, just shake the pan to mix. This is to prevent the bitterness of the *ampalaya* from taking over.

Sauté garlic in a little lard and put in the boiled vegetables. Season with vet-sin.
Note: If fish *bagoong* is used chop the fish and mix with the juice.

Laing

Serves: 6

⅓ kilo *alamang*
1 cup thick coconut milk
1 teaspoon salt
12 pieces small *gabi* leaves

1 cup diluted coconut milk from
second 'milking'
2 pieces *siling labuyo*

Mix *alamang* and ½ of the thick coconut milk. Season with salt. Place mixture by the tablespoon in each *gabi* leaf and wrap with ends tucked in. Arrange one on top of the other in an earthenware pot or *palayok*. Pour over diluted coconut milk and add *siling labuyo*. Simmer for 20 minutes, shaking the pot occasionally to prevent burning. Pour on the remaining thick coconut milk and continue cooking for about 10 minutes or until the sauce has thickened.

Rellenong talong or sili

Serves: 5

3 eggplants (7-8 inches long), or 3 large
bell peppers
3 tablespoons lard
4 cloves garlic
1 onion, chopped
2 medium tomatoes, chopped

¼ kilo pork, ground
salt and pepper to taste
vet-sin (monosodium glutamate)
2 eggs, stiffly beaten
extra lard for frying

Roast the eggplants, or bell peppers, in the broiler for 10 minutes, turning them occasionally so that all sides are broiled. When dark-brownish in color remove from heat and peel. Cut eggplant (or pepper) open lengthwise, and spread on plate.

Sauté the garlic, onion and tomatoes in lard, pressing them hard on the skillet. Add pork, season with salt, pepper and vet-sin. Cook until pork is done.

Remove some of the flesh from the eggplants then fill them (or peppers) with mixture. Dip stuffed eggplants (or peppers) into beaten egg and fry.

Chicken salad

(See photograph on page 75)

Serves: 10

2 apples
mayonnaise
¾ kilo diced cooked chicken
¾ cup peeled and diced cooked
carrots
3 cups peeled and diced cooked
potatoes

¾ cup finely diced celery
¾ cup finely diced pickles
1 cup diced green beans, half-cooked
salt, pepper and vinegar for
seasoning
red and green peppers for decoration

Peel and dice the apples and mix with a little mayonnaise Combine chicken, carrots, potatoes, celery, pickles and green beans. Season with salt, pepper and vinegar. Add the mayonnaise and the apple/mayonnaise mix. Arrange on a platter and decorate with red and green peppers to serve.

Avocado salad

Serves: 5

2 avocados, peeled and diced into
¾ inch pieces
½ can pineapple tidbits
1 cup mayonnaise
salt and sugar to taste
1 head Baguio lettuce
bottled Maraschino cherries (optional)

Mix avocado and pineapple with the mayonnaise. Season with salt and sugar. Serve on a bed of lettuce. Decorate with red cherries.

Tomato and crab salad

(See photograph on page 66)

Serves: 10

10 large Baguio tomatoes
salt and pepper for seasoning
2 cups crab meat
1 cup finely diced celery
½ small onion, chopped
½ teaspoon lemon juice

1 cup mayonnaise
extra salt and pepper for seasoning
1 head Baguio lettuce
2-3 hard boiled eggs
sprigs of parsley

Blanch the tomatoes in boiling water. Peel off the skin. Make a hole in the center, and remove some of the pulp. Season with salt and pepper and chill in the ice box.

Mix crab meat, celery, onion and lemon juice. Add a little mayonnaise and season with salt and pepper.

Fill the tomatoes with the mixture and cover with mayonnaise. Sprinkle with chopped hard boiled eggs and decorate with parsley. Place each tomato on a piece of Baguio lettuce to serve.

Vegetable salad

(See photograph on page 76)

Serves: 8

1 medium-sized can asparagus (for decor only)
pimento, cut into ½ x 3 inch strips
1 head Baguio or head lettuce, cut in wedges
6 medium-sized tomatoes (preferably Baguio), sliced crosswise
1 large cucumber (sides scored with a fork), sliced crosswise
dressing (see opposite)

Lay asparagus in straight strips in 4 sections from middle to rim on a round platter. Decorate crosswise with strips of *pimento* to make it look like a bundle. In between the asparagus bundles arrange alternately wedges of lettuce and slices of tomatoes and cucumber. Serve with Thousand Island Dressing.

Thousand Island Dressing
2 cups mayonnaise
1 tablespoon chopped celery
1 tablespoon chopped *pimento*
1 tablespoon chopped onion
2 tablespoons chopped pickles
5 tablespoons catsup
1 tablespoon Worcestershire sauce
a few drops of tabasco

Combine all the ingredients, mix thoroughly and serve separately in a bowl with salad.

Russian salad

Serves: 10-12

4 apples
mayonnaise
$^2/_3$ cup diced ham
$^2/_3$ cup diced cooked chicken
3 cups cubed cooked potatoes
1 cup cubed cooked carrots
¾ cup finely diced celery
vinegar, salt and pepper to taste
¾ cup cubed cooked beets
1 cup pineapple tidbits

Peel and dice apples and mix with a little mayonnaise. Combine ham, chicken, potatoes, carrots and celery. Marinate with a tablespoon of vinegar, salt and pepper. Add mayonnaise, beets, pineapple and apples mixed with mayonnaise.

Macaroni salad

Serves: 10

1 x 8 oz (250g) package Royal
macaroni
¼ kilo ham, cooked and diced
1 x 100 g can *pimento*
½ small onion, chopped
½ x 1 kilo chicken, cooked and diced
1 cup finely diced pickles
salt, pepper, vinegar and sugar to
taste
1½ cups mayonnaise
1 cup pineapple tidbits
½ cup grated Edam cheese (*queso
de bola*)

Boil macaroni in salted water until tender. Wash in cold water. Drain and cut into 1 inch pieces.

Combine macaroni with ham, *pimento*, onion, chicken and pickles. Season with salt, pepper, vinegar, and sugar. Add mayonnaise, pineapple and grated cheese.

Crema de Frutas (see recipe on page 96)

Gelatin (see recipe on page 98)

Desserts

Crema de frutas

(Refrigerator Cake)

(See photograph on page 93)

Serves: 12

Cake
6 eggs
¾ cup sugar
1¼ cups all-purpose flour
¼ teaspoon salt
4 tablespoons melted butter

Beat eggs until fluffy. Add sugar and continue beating until thick. Fold in dry ingredients and melted butter. Pour into 8 x 12 inches baking pan and bake at 325ºF for 15 minutes.

Cream filling
1 cup sugar
⅓ cup all-purpose flour
2¼ cups evaporated milk
¾ cup water
3 egg yolks
2 tablespoons butter

Other filling
1½ tablespoons unflavored gelatin
¼ cup water
1 No. 2 can 'fruits for salad'
1 cup water
juice of 2 *calamansi* or ½
tablespoon lemon juice
6 tablespoons sugar

Mix sugar and flour well. Add evaporated milk and water. Stir over heat until it thickens, then remove from heat and add egg yolks little by little. Stir over the fire again until it thickens. Remove once more from heat and when slightly cooled, add butter.

Soak the gelatin in the water. Drain the juice from 'fruits for salad'. To this juice add 1 cup of water, *calamansi* or lemon juice and sugar. Add gelatin and cook until it dissolves. Remove from heat and cool over ice until gelatin is set.

To make up cake

Cut the cake into ½ inch strips. Lay 5 or more of the strips on their sides close together in a dish. Cover with a layer of cream, some slices of fruit, then a layer of cake. Cover top with cream. Decorate with fruits (peaches, pineapple and cherries) and pour gelatin mixture over it. Allow to set in the ice box.

Gâteau le sans rival

Serves: 8-10

5 egg whites
1 cup sugar
1½ cups chopped *casoy*, or
almonds
½ teaspoon vanilla

Beat the egg whites until stiff. Add the sugar gradually and continue beating. Fold in the chopped nuts and the vanilla. Divide mixture into 4 or 5 well-greased and floured 9 inch diameter pans to make thin layers. Bake at 350°F until golden-brown. Remove at once and cool. With a spatula or knife, remove the now crisply baked contents of each pan. Stack on top of the other to form 4 to 5 layers.

Filling
¼ cup water
⅔ cup sugar
5 egg yolks
1 cup butter (8 oz)
½ cup chopped nuts

Boil water and sugar until it spins a thread. Pour mixture gradually over well-beaten egg yolks and continue beating until thick. Remove and chill in the ice box for 20 to 30 minutes. Cream the butter and add the chilled egg mixture.
Fill all layers and cover sides of cake. Sprinkle with chopped nuts.

Gelatin

(See photograph on page 94)

Serves: 8-10

4 tablespoons unflavored gelatin
1 No. 2½ can fruit cocktail
2 cups milk (fresh and undiluted)
½ cup water
1¾ cups sugar
juice of 2 *calamansi*
1 x 4 oz (125 grams) can Nestle's
cream
12 lady fingers
cherries for decorating

Soak powdered gelatin in juice drained from fruit cocktail. Heat the milk and the water. Add the gelatin and the sugar and cook until gelatin is melted. Put in *calamansi* juice and allow to cool. Add Nestle's cream and cool until just at the point of setting.

Arrange lady fingers in side ring moulds and pour the gelatin mixture over. Chill. When set, turn over on platter and decorate with cherries to serve.

Twenty-four hours fruit salad

Serves: 8

2 egg yolks
1 tablespoon lemon juice
4 tablespoons sugar
2 tablespoons butter
½ package (or 4 oz) marshmallows
1 No. 2½ can pineapple tidbits
1 No. 2½ can Royal Ann cherries **or**
1 No. 2½ can peaches
3 large oranges
1 bottle of Avoset cream

Dressing

Combine egg yolks, lemon juice and sugar in a double boiler. Stir until thick. Add the butter gradually and cool. Set aside.

Cut each marshmallow into four. Drain pineapple, cherries or peaches. Slice oranges, and cherries or peaches. Mix the fruits and marshmallows with the dressing.

Whip Avoset cream and add to the fruit mixture. Place in Tupperware or plastic container and keep in the freezer for 24 hours before serving.

Suspiros de macapuno

Makes: approx. 24 pieces

⅓ cup water
1¼ cups sugar
1½ cups mashed *macapuno*
rind of one *dayap*
4 egg yolks
meringue (see below)
½ cup (approx.) *casoy*
nuts chopped (for sprinkling)

Boil water and sugar until thick and syrupy. Add the *macapuno, dayap* rind and egg yolks. Cook over low heat until mixture forms a ball in the pan. Put 2 tablespoons of mixture each in soufflé cups. Cover with meringue and sprinkle with chopped *casoy* nuts.

Bake at 325°F for about 15 minutes until the meringue is hard on top.

Meringue
½ cup egg whites
1½ cups sugar

Beat the egg whites until stiff. Add the sugar gradually and continue beating until all sugar has been added and mixture is light and fluffy.

Masapan de pili

Makes: approx. 24-30 pieces

3 cups ground *pili* nuts
1½ cups sugar
4 egg yolks
rind of 1 *dayap*
1 x 14 oz (440 grams) can
condensed milk
2 tablespoons flour

Mix all ingredients except flour. Cook over a low heat, stirring continuously until mixture forms a ball in the pan. Add flour and continue cooking for 3 minutes more. Form into desired shapes usually 1½ inch diameter rounds, ½ inch thick, or ovals. Brush with egg yolk and broil until golden-brown.

Leche flan
(See photograph on page 111)

Serves: 8

1 cup sugar
8 egg yolks
2 egg whites
1 x 14 oz (397 g) can full cream
condensed milk
1 cup water
2 tablespoons sugar
rind of one *dayap*, grated

Caramelize sugar by stirring continuously over medium heat until melted. Pour into flan mould and tilt to cover the sides of pan up to two inches high.

Beat egg yolks and egg whites slightly. Add condensed milk, water, sugar, and *dayap* rind. Strain and pour mixture into the caramel-lined flan mould. Place mould in another bigger saucepan (*bain marie*) filled with 1 inch water. Bring to a boil and simmer for 40 minutes or until firm. Cool before removing flan from mould.

Apple pie

Serves: 8

2¼ cups all-purpose flour
½ teaspoon salt
12 tablespoons shortening
(Crisco or margarine)
6 tablespoons water
filling (see below)

Mix flour and salt in a bowl. Cut in the shortening with a pastry blender, or with two knives, until well blended. Add enough water to make into a smooth dough.

Set half of pastry aside and roll remainder out to ¼ inch thickness and line a 9 inch pie plate. Place filling in pastry case and cover with the other half of the pastry. Brush with milk and prick the whole surface with a fork. Bake at 400ºF for 20 minutes. Lower the temperature to 350ºF and bake for another 20 minutes.

Filling
8 to 10 apples
½ cup white sugar
½ cup brown sugar
2 tablespoons flour
1 teaspoon cornstarch
½ teaspoon cinnamon
2 tablespoons butter

Peel and core apples. Slice thinly. Mix white sugar, brown sugar, flour, cornstarch and cinnamon. Place inside pastry case in alternate layers of apples and sugar. Dot with butter. Cover with pastry and bake as directed above.

Caramel tartlets

Makes: approx. 60 pieces

Paste
2¼ cups flour
½ teaspoon salt
¾ cup Crisco or margarine
ice water

Mix the flour, salt and Crisco or margarine with a pastry blender. Add enough water to make a paste and roll. Line small tart boat moulds with pastry. Bake at 400ºF for about 15 minutes. Fill with caramel filling.

Filling
½ cup brown sugar
¾ cup white sugar
3 tablespoons flour
½ cup butter
¾ cup milk
3 egg yolks, slightly beaten

Caramelize brown sugar and white sugar. When melted, remove from the heat. Add flour, butter and milk. Cook over low heat until thick. Remove from heat. Add egg yolks gradually. Return to heat and cook for a further five minutes. Fill tart shells and top with meringue.

Meringue
⅓ cup egg whites
1 cup sugar

Beat egg whites until stiff. Add sugar gradually. Decorate top of tarts with this meringue, using a cake decorator with rose point No. 27. Bake in a slow oven (350ºF) until lightly browned.

Tocino del cielo

Makes: 24 moulds (1½ inch diameter)

3 cups sugar
⅓ cup butter
¾ cup water
16 egg yolks
rind of one *dayap*, grated

Caramelize 1 cup of sugar by stirring continuously over medium heat until melted. Line bottom of small *tocino del cielo* moulds thinly with caramelized sugar and butter sides.

Boil 2 cups sugar with the water until it spins a thread. Cool 2 minutes. Pour over the slightly beaten egg yolks and the rind. Add the butter. Strain and pour into moulds lined with caramelized sugar. Cook *tocino* (as in Leche flan recipe page 100) in *bain marie* for 15 minutes.

Cool and unmould into small soufflé cups.

Polvorones

Makes: approx. 80 pieces

4 cups all-purpose flour
¾ cup powdered milk
1½ cups sugar
1 cup butter

Toast flour in the broiler, or in a frying pan, until light brown. In a bowl, sift the toasted flour, powdered milk and sugar. Add the butter and mix thoroughly. Put mixture in standard *polvoron* mould and press out moulded. Wrap individual pieces in rectangles of multi-colored thin *papel de japon*. May be stored in a dry container or served immediately.

Orange gold cake

Serves: 10-12

Cake
¾ cup butter
1¼ cups sugar
8 egg yolks
2½ cups cake flour
3½ teaspoons baking powder
¼ teaspoon salt
3 tablespoons orange juice
½ cup milk

Filling
½ cup sugar
2 tablespoons flour
1 tablespoon cornstarch
½ cup water
¼ cup orange juice
1 teaspoon grated orange rind
1 egg yolk
1 tablespoon butter

Boiled frosting
1½ cups sugar
½ cup water
½ cup egg whites (cups because
some eggs are bigger than others
and this calls for exact
measurements)

Cake
Cream butter and sugar, then gradually add well-beaten egg yolks. Continue beating after each addition. Fold in flour, baking powder and salt alternately with orange juice and milk. Bake in 9 inch 2 layer cake pans at 325ºF for about 20 minutes.

Filling
Mix sugar, flour and cornstarch. Add water and cook over the fire until thick. Put in orange juice and orange rind and cook again until thick. Take mixture off the

fire, add slightly beaten egg yolk, little by little, return to heat and cook for about five minutes more. Allow filling mixture to cool, then fold in butter. Spread in between the two layers of cake.

Frosting
Boil sugar and water until it spins a thread. Beat egg whites stiffly then pour them into the syrup. Beat some more until slightly thick (about 7 minutes) or until a spreading consistency.

With a knife or spatula spread frosting over top and sides of cake.

Coffee pudding

Serves: 8

2 cups fresh milk
6 egg yolks
¾ cup sugar
2½ envelopes Knox (unflavored)
gelatin
6 egg whites
2 tablespoons instant coffee,
dissolved in 2 tablespoons hot water
½ teaspoon vanilla extract
1 cup whipped cream

Scald the milk in a saucepan. Set aside. Beat egg yolks slightly in a bowl. Add sugar, gelatin, and scalded milk. Pour into saucepan and stir over heat until mixture coats the spoon. **Note:** Mixture should not be thick.

Remove from heat, and place pan over ice water until cool. When cool, add coffee, vanilla and ½ cup whipped cream. Leave pan on ice so mixture thickens slightly. Meanwhile beat egg whites until stiff and add to mixture. Pour into a greased ring mould and place in the freezer.

When firm (approximately after one hour), turn over on a platter and decorate with remaining ½ cup whipped cream to serve.

Cream puffs

Makes: approx. 40 pieces

4 tablespoons butter
1 cup water
1 cup flour
pinch of salt
4 eggs
cream filling (see below)
caramel

Boil the butter and water. When bubbling add flour and salt. Over a low heat, beat until it forms a ball. Remove from heat and add eggs beating well after each addition. With an icing tube, make small balls 1 inch in diameter on a greased cookie sheet.

Bake at 400ºF for 30 minutes or until golden-brown. Remove from oven and cool. Fill cream filling and cover the top with caramel.

Cream filling
1 cup sugar
⅓ cup flour
2¼ cups evaporated milk
¾ cup water
5 egg yolks
2 tablespoons butter

Mix the sugar and flour thoroughly. Add milk and water. Stir over the heat until mixture thickens, then remove. Add egg yolks little by little. Stir over the fire again until mixture is thick. Remove from heat and when slightly cool, add butter.

Caramel
1½ cups sugar
½ cup water
¼ teaspoon cream of tartar

Melt 1 tablespoon of the sugar first (in order to give it color). When melted, add the rest of the sugar, the water and cream of tartar. Do not stir. Cook until mixture forms a ball when a small amount is dropped in cold water.

Lemon meringue pie

Serves: 8-10

1½ cups all-purpose flour
½ teaspoon salt
8 tablespoons shortening
a little ice water
lemon curd (see below)

Sieve flour and salt into a bowl. Work in shortening with two knives until evenly mixed. Add enough water to form mixture into a light smooth dough. Roll out dough on a floured board and line 9 inch pie mould.
　　Bake at 400ºF for 15 minutes or until brown. Fill with lemon curd.

Lemon curd
rind and juice of 1½ lemons
6 tablespoons butter
1 cup sugar
6 eggs

Meringue
3 egg whites
9 tablespoons sugar

Put the grated rind, lemon juice, butter, sugar and eggs in the top of double boiler. Stir over a low heat until mixture thickens and coats the spoon.
　　Cool mixture, then fill pie shell. Stiffly beat 3 egg whites, gradually add sugar. Then spread it on the top of the pie. Sprinkle with granulated sugar then bake at 350ºF for 10 minutes.
　　Cool and serve.

Lenguas de gato

Makes: about 50 pieces

½ cup butter
⅔ cup sugar
¼ cup egg whites (2 eggs)
1⅓ cup cake flour
¼ teaspoon salt
½ teaspoon vanilla

Cream butter and sugar. Add egg white gradually then fold in flour with salt. Add vanilla and stir mixture until smooth.

Use a cake decorating tube to form mixture into oblong shapes. Drop each shape onto a slightly greased cookie sheet. Bake at 375ºF for approximately 5-8 minutes or until light brown. Remove immediately and cool. Store in tightly covered containers.

Merienda

Pancit luglog

Serves: 10

6 tablespoons cooking oil
2 cloves garlic, minced
1 medium-sized onion, chopped
½ kilo shrimps, shelled
1 cup water in which ½ cup of
achuete has been soaked
salt and pepper to taste
3 cloves garlic, crushed
6 cups shrimp juice
patis
1 teaspoon vet-sin (monosodium glutamate)

¾ cup flour
½ kilo bijon (noodles)
½ kilo pork, boiled and sliced into
1 x ½ inch pieces
½ cup finely ground tinapa
½ cup powdered crisp sitsaron
calamansi for squeezing on pancit
3 eggs, hard boiled
3 spring onions, chopped
8 kamias, thinly sliced crosswise

Shrimp Mixture
Sauté 2 cloves garlic in 3 tablespoons cooking oil, add the onion and cook until soft. Add shrimps, ¼ cup of the achuete water and cook. Season with salt and pepper and set aside.

Palabok
In another pan heat 3 tablespoons cooking oil and add the crushed garlic and shrimp juice. Boil and stir continuously until fishy taste is removed. Add the rest of the achuete water (¾ cup). Season with patis, vet-sin and pepper. Thicken with flour dissolved in a little water. **Note:** This sauce should be thick.

Pancit
Boil 2 quarts of water in a saucepan. Put a handful of bijon into a sieve. Dip sieve into boiling water 1 minute and drain. Continue in this way until all the noodles have been cooked in boiling water. Pour noodles into a large plate. Cover with palabok. Top palabok with the shrimp mixture and sliced pork. Sprinkle with the flaked tinapa and sitsaron. Decorate with sliced hard boiled eggs, chopped spring onion, calamansi and sliced kamias if desired.

Leche Flan (see recipe on page 100)

Lily Sandwiches (see recipe opposite)

Lily sandwiches

(See photograph opposite)

Serves: 6

1 chicken breast, cooked
2 tablespoons chopped pickles
1 x 15 oz (470 g) can asparagus
spears
1 cup mayonnaise
salt and pepper to taste

1 large loaf of bread
butter for spreading
1 *pimento*, cut into fine strips
2 cucumber pickles, cut into fine
strips
parsley sprigs

Chop or mince chicken meat very finely. Drain asparagus spears. Mix chopped pickles, 5 chopped asparagus spears and mayonnaise. Season with salt and pepper and mix to a smooth paste. Cut bread into ¼ inch slices and remove crusts. Spread bread slices with butter then with the chicken mixture. Cut remaining asparagus spears into two lengthwise. Place an asparagus tip on one corner of bread slice with a slice of *pimento* and pickle on each side. Fold up like a lily and arrange on a round platter. Decorate with parsley.

Hot chocolate

Makes: 1 regular cup, or 2 demitasse

1 measure (*tablia*) Antonio Pueo chocolate
½ cup water
½ cup evaporated milk
½ to ¾ tablespoons sugar
Note: For every cup of chocolate use 1 measure of Antonio Pueo chocolate.

Place chocolate in a saucepan. Add water, evaporated milk, and sugar. First boil until chocolate dissolves then simmer until thick, stirring occasionally. Beat with a rotary or chocolate beater and pour into cups.

Ensaymadas

Makes: 6-12

½ cup lukewarm water
1 teaspoon sugar
1 level teaspoon yeast
1 cup all-purpose flour
6 egg yolks
9 tablespoons sugar
6 tablespoons butter

lard for kneading
2 cups flour
extra butter
1 cup grated cheese (preferably
queso de bola)
sugar

Put lukewarm water in a bowl. Add sugar and yeast. Let stand for 10 minutes then add all-purpose flour and mix with a wooden spoon. Cover with a towel and let rise in a warm place until double its bulk (about 40 minutes to 1 hour).

Add egg yolks, sugar and butter to flour mixture. Add to this the 2 cups of flour and knead with lard. Let rise again in warm place (about 3 hours) until double its bulk.

Divide into 6 to 12 portions. Roll each portion to ¼ inch thick on a greased board. Spread with butter and sprinkle with grated cheese. Roll up, starting from one end and twisting like a knot. Place each roll into an *ensaymada* mould lined with wax paper and greased with lard.

Keep in a warm place until each roll doubles its bulk (about 4 hours). Bake at 350ºF for 10 minutes or until light brown. Brush with butter and sprinkle with grated cheese and sugar.

Guinatan halo-halo

Serves: 8-10

1 cup *malagkit* rice
3 medium-sized *camotes*
7 *saba* bananas, sliced crosswise
1 cup *nangka* meat, cut into strips
1 teaspoon anise
¾-1 cup sugar, to taste

5 cups coconut milk (second extraction)
1 cup thick coconut milk (first extraction)
puto maya (see opposite)

Soak the rice in water overnight. Grind the rice to a stiff dough (*galapong*) and form two-thirds of it into small balls, the size of the *garbanzos*. Dilute the remaining *galapong* in water and set aside. Cut the *camotes* into ½ inch cubes and boil in the coconut milk of the second extraction. Drop in the m*alagkit* balls, bananas, *nangka*, anise and sugar. Simmer until cooked. Thicken with the reserved *galapong* diluted in water. Top each plate with the thick coconut milk and serve with *puto maya*.

Puto Maya
2 cups *malagkit* rice
3½ cups water
½ grated coconut
sugar for sprinkling

Boil rice in water. When cooked, mould in cups. Top with grated coconut and sprinkle with sugar.

Guinatan mongo

Serves: 8

½ cup *mongo*
1 cup *malagkit* rice
1 cup thick coconut milk (first extraction)
5 cups coconut milk (second extraction)
¾ cup sugar, to taste
½ tablespoon salt

Roast *mongo* in frying pan until brown. Break the grains using a rolling pin. Remove the hull, wash *malagkit* rice and boil with *mongo* in the second extraction of coconut milk. Add roasted *mongo*, stirring occasionally. When rice is cooked add sugar and salt. Top with thick coconut milk.

Ukoy

Serves: 5

1 cup small fresh shrimps
1 cup cornstarch
½ teaspoon baking soda
½ teaspoon baking powder
½ teaspoon vet-sin (monosodium glutamate)
½ teaspoon salt
1 cup water
lard for deep frying

Remove shrimp whiskers and the sharp outer shells of the heads. Wash and set aside. Sift dry ingredients together in a bowl. Add water and stir. Put in the shrimps.

Heat lard in deep pan or small native frying pan. Drop in mixture by the tablespoon. With cooking spoon, gather together particles that tend to separate in the lard and form patties 2-3 inches in diameter. Fry until brown. Drain in large strainer or on paper towels.

Serve on a platter with a bowl of vinegar, salt, pepper and 1 crushed clove of garlic for dipping.

Pinwheel sandwiches

1 cup grated cheese
4 tablespoons butter
⅓ cup catsup
1 loaf sliced bread

Mix all the ingredients together and spread on bread sliced lengthwise. Roll up like a jellyroll, wrap in wax paper and chill in the ice box. When firm cut into thin slices.

Sio pao

Serves: 12

Dough
1½ cups lukewarm water
2 tablespoons sugar
1 teaspoon dry yeast
4½ cups all-purpose flour
1 tablespoon baking powder
½ cup sugar
3 tablespoons pork lard
filling (see below)

Into lukewarm water place 2 tablespoons sugar and yeast, and let stand for 10 minutes. Mix flour, baking powder, remaining sugar and lard. Add this mixture to the yeast mixture. Knead until smooth. Let rise for 2 hours.

Divide dough into 24 to 32 small balls. Arrange balls on the table and fill each with a tablespoon of filling. Place each filled *sio pao* on a 2 inch square of wax paper. Let stand for ½ hour.

Arrange *sio pao* in a steamer lined with cheesecloth or towel. Steam for 15 minutes.

Filling
2 tablespoons lard
6 cloves garlic
1 kilo pork shoulder (*kasim*) cut into
large chunks
2 medium-sized onions, sliced
4 tablespoons soy sauce
3 tablespoons sugar
2 tablespoons seafood sauce, **or**
1 teaspoon oyster sauce

Heat lard in a pan and sauté garlic. Add pork and brown lightly. Add all the remaining ingredients and cook until tender. Remove pork and dice it into ½ inch cubes. Return pork to mixture. Add seafood sauce, or oyster sauce, and use filling as above.

Cassava bibingka

Serves: 6-8

2 eggs
1¼ cups coconut milk
1 cup sugar
2 tablespoons melted butter
¼ cup evaporated milk
3 tablespoons grated cheese
½ cup shredded *buko*
1 cup grated *cassava*
banana leaves
egg yolk for brushing
native cheese (*kesong puti*), sliced
finely
sugar

Beat the eggs. Add coconut milk, sugar, butter, evaporated milk, grated cheese, *buko* and *cassava*.
Pour into a 11 x 7 x 1½ inch pan lined with banana leaves wilted in fire first. Bake at 375ºF degrees for 40 minutes. Brush with egg yolk and decorate with slices of native cheese and sugar to taste. Bake for another 10 minutes.

Huevos à la donesa

Serves: 8

8 hard boiled eggs
1 can *azteco*, or *matapan* sardines
4 tablespoons butter
2 tablespoons chopped spring onions
4 tablespoons salad oil
2 teaspoons vinegar
salt to taste
pimento, cut into rounds
sliced stuffed olives for garnish

Cut eggs lengthwise. Remove the yolks and pass them through a strainer. Mash the sardines but discard accompanying vegetables. Mix the sardines with the mashed egg yolks and add the butter, onions, oil, vinegar and salt.

Fill egg whites with the mixture. Cut halved eggs again into two, making 4 slices out of one egg. Decorate with *pimento* or sliced stuffed olives. Serve for cocktails.

Nougatines

Makes: 45-50 pieces

Short Crust
1½ cups all-purpose flour
3 egg yolks
pinch of salt
3 rounded tablespoons sugar
3 ounces (90 grams) butter

Filling
4 tablespoons butter
⅓ cup sugar
1 egg, beaten
½ cup cake crumbs
½ cup coarsely chopped almonds
or *casoys*

Put flour on a board or slab. Make a well in the center and pour in egg yolks, salt, sugar and butter. Work center ingredients into a smooth paste and quickly work in the flour.

Roll dough with rolling pin until ⅛ inch thick. Lay flattened dough on board or table. Cut with boat-shaped fluted cutter. Take boat moulds and line insides with the cut dough with fluted sides.

Filling
Cream butter, sugar and egg. Add cake crumbs, almond or *casoys* and cream further. Half-fill each tart shell with this mixture, sprinkle with *casoys* and bake at 375°F for about 15 minutes, or until golden-brown.

Toasted sandwiches

Makes: 20 pieces

¼ cup butter
1 cup grated cheese
½ of 200 grams can *pimento*
1 loaf sliced bread

Cream butter, grated cheese and finely chopped *pimento*. Spread on bread, roll and fasten with toothpick. Toast in the broiler.

Hot cakes

Makes: approx. 12-14 small (4 inch diameter) cakes

4 eggs
1 cup milk
2 tablespoons melted shortening
1¾ cups cake flour
3 teaspoons baking powder
½ teaspoon salt
2 tablespoons sugar

Separate eggs, beat yolks slightly and add milk and shortening. Mix dry ingredients in a bowl. Add the liquid ingredients and mix. **Note:** This mixture should be lumpy. Beat egg whites until stiff. Fold into the first mixture.

Drop by the spoonful onto a slightly greased iron skillet until cooked then turn once. Serve with home-made syrup (see below), maple syrup or honey.

Syrup
⅓ cup water
1 cup brown sugar (packed)

Boil water and sugar together for 5 minutes to form syrup.

Petits fortunes

Makes: 40 pieces

¾ cup chopped *casoys*
2 tablespoons all-purpose flour
½ cup sugar
2 egg yolks, slightly beaten
2 tablespoons heavy cream
⅓ cup butter, melted
1 egg white, stiffly beaten
powdered sugar and glacé cherries
for decoration

Mix thoroughly the dry ingredients in a bowl. Make a well in the center and add egg yolks, cream and melted butter. Mix until well blended and add egg white.
    Pour into 1¼ inch diameter fluted paper cups and bake at 350ºF for 12-15 minutes. Sprinkle a small amount of powdered sugar through a fine strainer on each petit fortune. Decorate individually with a cherry to serve.

Madelines

Makes: 24 pieces

3 eggs
½ cup sugar
1 cup cake flour
4 ounces (125 grams) melted butter
½ teaspoon vanilla

Put eggs and sugar in a bowl and beat until thick. Fold in flour and melted butter. Add vanilla and fill madeline moulds. If madeline moulds not available use frilled paper cups 3 inches in diameter. Bake at 375ºF for about 15 minutes.

Churros

Makes: 24 pieces

1 cup water
½ teaspoon salt
2 teaspoons olive oil
1 cup cake flour
cooking oil (deep fat)
sugar for sprinkling

Boil water with salt, and olive oil. Pour into the cake flour and mix well. Pass through a pastry bag or *churera*, piping through the icing tube in a loop formation as illustrated. Fry quickly in hot oil until light brown. Sprinkle with sugar and serve with hot chocolate (see page 113).

Guinatan maiz

Serves: 8-10

1 cup *malagkit* rice
5 cups coconut milk (2nd extraction)
1 can No. 2 creamed corn **or**
1 cup young corn, scraped from
the cob and mashed
¾ cup sugar, to taste
1 teaspoon salt
1 cup thick coconut milk (1st
extraction)

Wash *malagkit* rice. Boil in second coconut milk extraction, stirring occasionally until soft. Put in the corn. Add sugar and salt. Pour thick coconut milk in and cook for 3 minutes.

Pickles

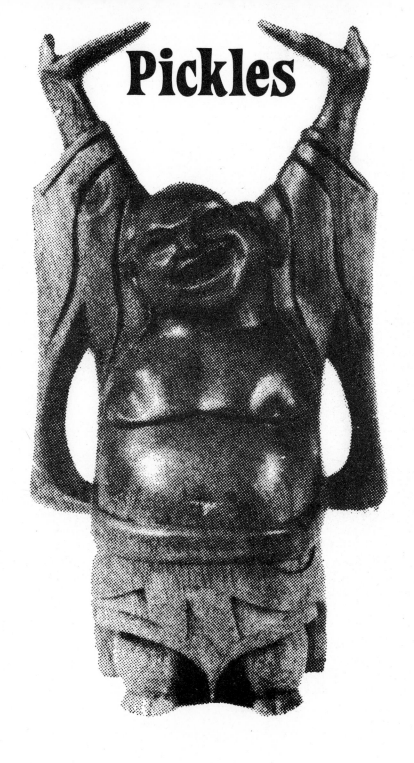

Papaya pickles

Makes: 24 ounces

4 cups grated green *papaya*
2 cups vinegar
1 cup sugar
2 teaspoons salt
20 small native onions, sliced finely
2 red bell peppers, sliced finely
1 piece ginger (about 1 inch square)
sliced finely
1 head garlic, sliced finely

Squeeze *papaya* to remove juice. Wash *papaya* and drain, then set aside. Boil 1 cup vinegar, ½ cup sugar and 1 teaspoon salt. Add the *papaya* and boil for about 10 minutes. Add onions and peppers and boil once. Discard liquid by draining.

Boil remaining vinegar, sugar and salt. Add *papaya*, onions and peppers. Put in ginger and garlic. Remove from heat and cool.

Mango chutney

Makes: 36 ounces (each mango fills one 6 oz (185 g) bottle)

6 large green mangoes
syrup (see opposite)
2 green bell peppers, cut into thin
strips
2 red bell peppers, cut into thin strips
2 pieces hot peppers, cut into thin
strips
1 head garlic, cut into thin strips
1 ginger, cut into thin strips
20 small native onions, sliced finely
⅓ cup raisins

Syrup
¼ cup vinegar
1 cup sugar   per mango
¾ teaspoon salt

Peel and thinly slice mangoes into 3 inch long pieces. Set aside.
   Boil vinegar, sugar and salt. When the mixture thickens, add the mangoes. Cook until mangoes are transparent. Put in peppers, garlic, ginger and onions and boil for about ten minutes. Add the raisins. Pour the mixture into bottles while still hot, and cover. **Note:** Chutney will keep longer if sterilized by putting bottled chutney in boiling water for 20 minutes.

Pickles for Saté Babi

Fills two 24 ounce bottles

3 tablespoons Wesson oil
1 teaspoon chopped garlic
2 tablespoons chopped onions
2 tablespoons chopped peanuts or
pili nuts
½ cup brown sugar
½ teaspoon salt
1½ cups native vinegar
½ cup water
2 small carrots, pared and cut into
2 x ½ inch pieces
1 large green cucumber, cut into
2 x ½ inch pieces
⅛ kilo whole native onions
(scallions), peeled
¼ kilo green beans (habichuelas),
boiled and cut into 2 inch pieces
10 medium-sized green peppers
(pointed tip, panigang variety)

Heat oil in saucepan. Add garlic, onions and nuts. Cook for five minutes or until onions are transparent. Add brown sugar, salt, vinegar and water. Boil for 5 minutes.
   Strain liquid, then pour on carrots, cucumber, onions, green beans and green peppers. Let stand for two hours before serving.

Glossary

AA-GAUGAU brand of cornstarch (*gaugau* is cornstarch)

ACHUETE red *anatto* seeds used for food coloring

ADOBO pork, chicken, fish or vegetables cooked basically in vinegar with garlic and pepper. Adobo is the name of the dish as well as the style of cooking

ALAMANG small shrimps usually used for *bagoong*

ALIMASAG crabs with pointed shell, spotted

AMPALAYA bitter melons

APAHAP sea bass

APULID water chestnuts

BAGOONG salted and fermented small shrimps or fish (like *bagoong alamang*)

BAIN MARIE a type of double boiler or small container in a large pan of water

BAKE cook in oven at a certain temperature and for a particular length of time

BANGUS milkfish, most popular pond raised fish

BATTER a mixture of flour, liquid and other ingredients, which can be poured

BAY LEAF laurel; the aromatic leaf of the bay tree, used for seasoning

BID-BID Hawaiian ten pounder; fish with sticky flesh, used for *bola bola*

BIJON fine white rice noodles used for *pancit*

BLANCH to whiten; to remove skin by scalding; to immerse in hot, then in cold water

BLEND combine ingredients evenly

BOUILLON a stock made of veal or beef bones; giblets and vegetable flavoring; it can also be made from vegetables only

BREADCRUMBS made by pounding and straining toasted or very stale bread

BROIL cook on rack or skewer in oven or over direct flame

BUKO young coconut with very soft flesh

BUTUAN seedy variety of banana

CALAMANSI native lemons

CAMARRON shrimp

CAMOTES sweet potatoes

CARAMEL sugar cooked in a little water and glucose; sugar cooked to a dark brown without water

CASOY cashew nut

CASSAVA root crop of sweet potato variety commonly used in native cakes

CASSEROLE a heat-proof baking dish

CHICHARO sweet peas

CHOP cut into small pieces with a heavy knife

CHORIZO DE BILBAO Spanish sausage

CHURERA pastry tube used specifically for *churros*

CLAVOS DE COMER cloves

DALAGANG BUKID species of fresh water fish

DAYAP local species of aromatic lime

DREDGE to coat with flour or sugar

EVAPORATED MILK for these recipes, use pure evaporated milk

FILLETS strips of boneless fish; thick slices of meat

FOIE GRAS goose liver paste

GABI taro

GALAPONG dough of ground rice and water made to stand overnight

GARBANZOS chickpeas

GINGER JUICE pound ginger root, add water and extract juice

GOTO tripe

GUISADO sautéed

HABICHUELAS green beans

HALAAN clams

KABILUGAN flank

KANGKONG swamp cabbage

KASIM pork shoulder

KENCHIE beef (hind shank)

KESONG PUTI native cheese

KINCHAY Chinese celery

LABONG bamboo shoots

LABUYO see *siling labuyo*

LAPAY pork spleen

LAPULAPU spotted grouper

LECHON whole roasted pig

LUMPIA spring roll

MACAPUNO freak coconut full to the brim with soft meat

MALAGKIT glutinous rice

MARINADE a mixture (of vinegar, soy sauce, herbs, wine, peppercorns, or whatever) used for soaking poultry meat or fish

MASHED crushed with a fork to soften consistency

MINCE chop very finely

MONGO mung beans

NGO-YONG all spice powder bought from Chinese grocers

OKRA tall plant bearing mucilaginous seed-pods used as a vegetable and for thickening soups

OREGANO a stem-like herb used for seasoning particularly in pasta dishes, sauces and meat marinades

OYSTER SAUCE Cantonese sauce made from ground dried oyster and salt

PALABOK garnishing

PANCIT Filipino dish of Chinese origin, made mainly from noodles

PAN DE SAL most common type of bread buns available in the Philippines

PANIGANG any ingredients used in sour soups

PAPEL DE JAPON brightly colored thin rice paper.

PATA pig's feet

PATIS fish sauce; concentrated juice of salted fish

PATOLA variety of gourd, sometimes called bottle gourd

PECHAY Chinese cabbage

PIGUÉ (pigi) fresh pork ham

PILI *pili* nuts

PINA pineapple

PINIPIG young rice roasted and pounded

PUSIT squids

QUESO DE BOLA Edam cheese, ball-shaped with red rind

QUESONG PUTI *See Kesong puti*

RICE WASHING or RICE WATER water obtained from washing uncooked rice for the second or third time.

SABA cooking variety of banana

SALITRE potassium nitrate commonly known as saltpeter; preserves and colors foods such as hams, sausages and dried meats

SAUTÉ fry in a small amount of fat

SCALLIONS native onions

SHELL remove the outer coat of shellfish, nuts or seeds

SHRED cut into thin strips

SHRIMP JUICE obtained by pounding the head of shrimps, adding water and straining

SILI from the Mexican "chili" (chili peppers)

SILING LABUYO or *siling pasiti*; very small, very hot red or green peppers

SIMMER cook in fluid at a temperature below boiling point

SINGKAMAS turnip; often used as a substitute for water chestnuts

SITAO string bean

SITAW string beans

SITSARO or *chicharo*; sweet pea

SITSARON pork crackling

SOTANGHON transparent variety of rice noodle

SOUFFLÉ CUPS used in *Tocino del Cielo* (diameter is 1 to 1½ inches); and *Suspiros de Macapuno* (diameter is 2 to 3 inches)

STEAM cook in a sealed container over boiling liquid so that steam heat does the actual cooking

TABLIA solid chocolate for making breakfast chocolate drink

TAINGANG DAGA black wood ear (variety of mushroom)

TALABA oysters

TALONG eggplant

TAPA, TAPA CUT dried meat. Tapa cut is the cut used for drying, but also can be used fresh

TAUSI fermented soybean curd

TIMBALE any kind of food baked in a custard base

TINAPA smoked fish

TOYO or soy sauce; black salty sauce made from soy beans

UBOD heart of palm; pith of coconut trunk

UNTOSINSAL leaf lard

VET-SIN a brand of monosodium glutamate (in the Philippines, interchangeable with each other)

MOULDS AND PASTRY CUTTERS

FLUTED CUTTER aluminium or tin pastry cutter used for cutting boat shaped tartlets. About 4½ inches long and 2½ inches wide in the middle, slightly tapering at both ends. Edges are fluted.

MADELINE MOULD aluminium or tin pastry mould, slightly similar to a sea shell shape. About 2½ inches long and 1¾ inches wide.

POLVORON MOULD aluminum or tin mould used in making polvoron. Usually round or oblong in shape, ¾ inch deep.

TART SHELLS boat shaped aluminum molds used for making certain pastries. About 4 inches long and 1¼ inches at the widest point in middle, with both ends tapered.

Index